Rigorous Grace

Rigorous Grace

Practicing the Life of Jesus

PRESTON GILLHAM

PUBLICATION™

Published and printed in the United States of America
by Bonefish Publication

Fort Worth, Texas

For bulk purchase discounts, please contact
Bonefish Publication: info@bonefishpublication.com.

For further information about *Rigorous Grace*, other works by the author,
his blog, or to contact the author about speaking engagements, or his
guidance work, please visit: PrestonGillham.com

Unless otherwise noted, all scripture references are from the
Holy Bible, New American Standard Version (NASB),
Lockman Foundation, La Habra, CA. 1975.

Library of Congress Control Number: 2022902953

ISBN: 978-0-9845103-7-5

PUBLICATION™

Perspectives on *Rigorous Grace*

"Fantastic!!!" --Harvey

"Your message is relative and spot on. Keep up the good work." --Paul

"You are an important voice in a time like no other in my lifetime." --Joanie

"What a gifted writer you are." --Cindy

"You have unique insight from God." --Marilu

"This is good, really good." --Hank

"You are hitting home run after home run!" --Vic

"Excellent." --Erik

"EXCELLENT, EXCELLENT, EXCELLENT!" --Max

"Your work and your words offer insight, hope, and enough depth insomuch that I never feel like I'm wading through your story. TRUTH written, HOPE perceived, LOVE on pages. Keep fighting the good fight." --Gigi

"Thank you for your writing—it encourages me greatly!" --Nancy

"Thanks so much, Preston, for using your gifts and amazingly talented writing ability to cut through all the cacophony to the heart of the matter!" --Meredith

FOCI

"We learn by practice and become an athlete of God."

Martha Graham

"To practice any art, no matter how well or badly, is a way to make your soul grow. So do it."

Kurt Vonnegut

"Discipline is consistency of action."

Jim Collins

"The essential thing 'in heaven and earth' is that there should be a long obedience in the same direction."

Friedrich Nietzsche

"Through discipline comes freedom."

Aristotle

For additional works
by Preston Gillham
or to subscribe to his blog,
visit:

www.PrestonGillham.com

Table of Contents

DEDICATION

To the church of Jesus Christ, corporate and individual, my brothers and sisters in the faith:

May the eyes of your heart be enlightened so that you know the hope of God's calling, the glorious riches that are your inheritance as a saint, and the surpassing greatness of His power toward you, in you, and through you as you practice the life of Jesus Christ.

Prologue

For the last two decades I've been exploring why the church is losing its voice in society. From both inside and outside, the critique of the church is that it and its message are no longer relevant.[1]

That is a grim criticism and an indicting charge.

What's going on? Does this matter? What do we do to remedy this charge of irrelevancy?

---

[1] Researchers from Barna to Gallop to Pew, et al, and journalists from *Time* to *USA Today*, et al, have explored the church's decline. First, they defined "committed Believers" as those adherents to Christianity who desire for their faith to be relevant seven days a week. Once identified, committed Believers were asked why they left the church. Three outcomes emerged: 1) These Believers made it clear that they had not left the faith. They were just as committed as ever to their walk with Christ Jesus—it's just that their Christian life no longer included participation in an organized church. 2) The stated reason for committed Believer's departure from the church is that the church and its message are no longer relevant, i.e., applicable seven days a week. This departure accounts for the sharp rise in those called "none's" when assessing the state of religious participation in America. 3) A high percentage of committed Believers still participating in church indicate that they attend for the sake of their children, not because they find church relevant. These church members' children, as well as new converts to the faith who participate in church, are fewer in number than the older church members who are dying. Thus, the church is in a numerical death spiral. Compounded with society's hostile view of evangelicalism, the church is in crisis.

The church—individual and corporate—has lost its relevance because we have failed in our fundamentals. We've grown lax in our dedication to the practices that help us realize and obtain our heart's desire: to know God personally and walk effectively and meaningfully with Him daily. As our practices degraded, we—the church—turned inward, thus diminishing our light and influence in society, and in time, lost confidence that our faith as presented is relevant.

By relevant, we mean not only the conviction that what you believe about Christ and Christianity is true, but that your belief is substantive enough and effective enough that you know how to apply your faith every day of the week.

While we know a great deal *about* God and what He's done for us, it is only through diligent dedication to the practice of the spiritual disciplines that we position ourselves to truly *know* God. Given this, a return to our fundamentals will precede our return to relevance in society and influence within culture.

Our message as the church is the Gospel. That's certainly not irrelevant. Our delivery is a smorgasbord of ministries. Yet, no program, tactic, appeal, gimmick, or series is retaining dedicated Believers, let alone attracting those outside the family of faith.

The Wall Street Journal published an article by Ian Lovett on December 15, 2021. The first paragraph after the byline reads: "The percentage of Americans who identify as Christians now stands at 63%, down from 65% in 2019 and from 78% in 2007. Meanwhile, 29% of Americans now identify as having no religion, up from 26% in 2019 and 16% in 2007, when Pew began tracking religious identity."[2]

Later in the same article, the Barna Group is referenced estimating that in-person attendance at church is 30% to 50% lower than it was prior to the pandemic.[3]

It's also concerning to note, "A previous Pew survey, in January, found that a third of Americans said their faith had grown stronger during the pandemic—the highest share of any developed country. But overall, religious engagement trended downward at roughly the same rate as before the pandemic."[4]

These are not good numbers. In fact, there are no good numbers for the church. It's a bit counterintuitive to think of the organized church as a business, but there's merit in asking: Can a declining business that loses an additional 30%-50% of its customers in eighteen months survive?

It's tempting to say the world is so dark that the Gospel can't break through. I'm not buying that explanation and neither is the long story of Christian history.

It's also tempting to say we need one more program, one more emphasis, one more study. I'm not buying that either. The church has more information and access to more spiritual teaching than at any time in history.

It's also tempting to say ministers are not hip enough, not current enough. If a minister would use more technology, untuck his shirt tail, comb his hair differently, utilize a

[2] Lovett, Ian. "More Americans Left Religion During the Pandemic." *FoxNews.com* and *WSJ.com*. December 15, 2021. https://www.foxnews.com/lifestyle/americans-left-religion-during-covid-pandemic?cmpid=prn_newsstand
[3] Ibid.
[4] Ibid.

smoke machine, change the lighting on stage.... I'm not buying this line of critique either.

Whether it is business, athletics, an area of expertise, a hobby, dental health, or the spiritual life, everything human is dependent upon fundamental practices. Without variation, when fundamental failure occurs, it is because a fundamental was lost, broken, botched, or ignored.

No, the church does not need something more to regain its relevance. The church needs to return to its fundamental practices: those behaviors identified as the spiritual disciplines.

We are deemed irrelevant by those within and those outside the church because our fundamentals are pithy, poorly executed, and partially practiced. The church has lost its voice and influence within society because the church has lost its way. This is a systems issue, not a quantitative or qualitative issue. Godin notes, "If you're not working on your system, you're not going to improve it."[5]

I need to forewarn you: There is controversy and pushback to any consideration of the spiritual disciplines.

But pushback is common to all discipline: It's not fun, convenient, easy.... Rationalization, excuses, justification. All discipline for the moment is hard, but discipline is necessary to achieve a desired goal that is noble, lofty, and inspiring.[6]

This particular controversy over the place of the disciplines in daily life asserts that practicing the spiritual disciplines

---

[5] Godin, Seth. "Effort Toward Quality." *Seths.blog.* January 4, 2022. https://seths.blog/2021/10/effort-toward-quality/
[6] Cf.: Hebrews 12:11.

is legalistic—legalism being the notion that you can improve your standing with God, gain more of His acceptance, further sanctify yourself, or enhance your justification with Him by what you do.

Let's be clear: While performance -based acceptance with God is common teaching within Christianity, it is bad theology. In fact, it's heretical. Legalism has no biblical merit because it diminishes the finished work of Jesus Christ.

Your standing with God is Jesus-based. Period. Any addition or subtraction to the completed work of Christ is heresy. In Christ alone, through faith alone, is your redemption.

Rigorous Grace is not a book advocating for legalism. Practicing the spiritual disciplines is not legalistic. In fact, Dietrich Bonhoeffer said, "This [practice of the disciplines] is not 'legalism'; it is orderliness and fidelity."[7]

Let the critics rant. To argue that practicing the spiritual disciplines is legalistic is simplistic and shortsighted. In fact, any dismissal of practicing the spiritual disciplines contributes to the fundamental problem the church faces.

If all you have as a Christian is Christian belief, you are no better off than a demon. They too believe—and shudder, the Bible states.[8] For your faith in Christ to be relevant, your belief must be applied. Rigorously. If your faith is not applied, if grace remains an ideal and mercy is only a theological construct, then you are on your own when it

---

[7] Bonhoeffer, Dietrich. *Life Together*. HarperOne, an imprint of Harper Collins Publishers. New York, NY. 1954.
[8] Cf.: James 2:19.

comes to living life. The Bible puts it this way: "Faith without works [behavior] is useless."[9]

Faith that lacks corresponding behavior is not useless because your faith is false, unreliable, or not true. It's useless because faith that isn't applied does you no earthly good. It gains you access to eternity, but it is not useful in your daily life, thereby making it irrelevant, God distant, Christ's work on your behalf theoretical, and the power of the Holy Spirit inert.

Faith without works. Grace not applied. Mercy not implemented. These great tenets of the faith are useless theological truths until you implement them. This requires practice, discipline, and focus on fundamentals.

Just as Jesus Christ came to give you life eternal, He also came to live His life through you. If the reality of Christ in you is not infusing and affecting all aspects of your existence, then you have a faith, a theology of grace, and an adherence to God's mercy that is useless at worst, unreliable at best, irrelevant in any case.

This simply must not—cannot—be reflective of the Gospel of Jesus Christ. Yet, the accusation against the church stands. Irrelevant!

---

[9] James 2:20 (Cf.: 2:14-26).

Terminology

Church: those individuals who are Christians; Believers whose eternal salvation is secured through faith alone, in Jesus Christ alone; the Body of Christ, God's family, God's children; a living organism of individuals and groups of people made alive together through the life of Christ; the people of God, a living organism as opposed to denominational and nondenominational organizations identified as churches.

Discipline: orderly, prescribed training expected to produce a specific character, conduct, or pattern of behavior; the exercise of self-control.

Fundamentals: the foundational, central, essential structures necessary to determine existence or function; the essential components; central, ingrained, deep-rooted characteristics of great significance.

Grace: the free and unmerited favor of God personified in Jesus Christ.

Practice: to perform habitually; to acquire or polish a skill; to drill repeatedly in order to become better at a skill or assent and make that behavior an ordinary part of life.

Rigorous: the quality of being thorough, accurate, demanding; a diligent and determined application.

Spiritual: everything pertaining to life and godliness.

Thus

Practicing the spiritual disciplines: the regular exercise and effort to habitually implement the essential components of Christianity into your life; making your behavior reflective of spiritual reality; the means by which your faith becomes habitual and incorporated into all aspects of your life.

Rigorous grace: the life of Jesus Christ made relevant and vibrant in all aspects of your daily life.

ONE

Practicing Discipline

"

"Please use some other word than discipline in your book."

Quote from friend

Within the community of faith, discipline has fallen out of favor, while in the secular community, those who coach and inspire discipline are sought after by those endeavoring to live more effective, fulfilling lives.

Numbers for the faith community are in sharp decline. Numbers for those seeking to learn discipline are skyrocketing.

As I have shared pre-publish pages of *Rigorous Grace* with advance readers, I've heard, "You can't say discipline." "You've got to get rid of that word." "I can't get past the idea of discipline." "Isn't there another word you can use—another way other than discipline?"

Meanwhile, as of the First Quarter 2022, Jocko Willink's black and white, grainy video, no nonsense— "It's Monday, ya'll. Go get some! Discipline equals freedom!"—podcast had over a million followers.[10] His Instagram, which each day pictures Jocko's digital watch within a few minutes of his 4:30 AM wake-up, boasted 2.3 million followers.[11] Together with Leif Babin, their book *Extreme Ownership*, which preaches the power of taking personal responsibility, is a #1 best-seller. Out of 22,000+ Amazon reviews, the book receives 4.8 stars with 86% of reviewers giving the book a 5-star rating.[12]

Entire industries are devoted to the rewards of practicing discipline and are made applicable across every field of human engagement. Physical, mental, emotional, willful, and yes, spiritual life are dependent upon discipline to establish resilient, flexible, satisfying, meaningful, application to life.

As noted in this book's Foci by the legendary Jim Collins, "Discipline is consistency of action."

Action begins with sincere belief and is undergirded by intent, but these alone are insufficient to make any conviction, including spiritual conviction, useful to life. Scripture notes that even the demons believe and shudder,[13] and we all know that the road to hell is paved with good intention. As the Apostle James noted two millennia ago, and as modern researchers are reporting, a belief system that isn't or can't be applied to life and living is deemed irrelevant.[14]

Speaking to a useless, irrelevant faith and how to avoid such an unfortunate conclusion, Peter opens his second book citing the magnificence of God's grace—a grace so profound that it makes us partakers of God's nature. But knowing that theology alone

---

[10] Cf.": *JockoPodcast.com*.

[11] Cf.: *Instagram.com/JockoWillink/*.

[12] Cf.: *Amazon.com*. Accessed, 8 February 2022. https://www.amazon.com/Extreme-Ownership-audiobook/dp/B015TM0RM4/ref=sr_1_1?keywords=extreme+ownership&qid=164433 1316&s=books&sprefix=extreme%2Cstripbooks%2C101&sr=1-1

[13] Cf.: James 2:19.

[14] Cf.: James 2:20.

is insufficient for the tumult of the times, he writes, "Now for this very reason also, applying all diligence, in your faith supply..." and he proceeds to list what we are to supply: moral excellence, knowledge, self-control, perseverance, and so forth—the very qualities discipline produces. By the time Peter finishes his introduction, he has spoken multiple times of diligence, excellence, practice, clear vision, truth, establishment, and determination, noting in verse eight, "If these qualities are yours and are increasing, they render you neither *useless* nor unfruitful in the knowledge of Jesus Christ" (emphasis mine). Here's Peter's quote:

> Simon Peter, a bond-servant and apostle of Jesus Christ,
>
> To those who have received a faith of the same kind as ours, by the righteousness of our God and Savior, Jesus Christ: ² Grace and peace be multiplied to you in the knowledge of God and of Jesus our Lord; ³ seeing that His divine power has granted to us everything pertaining to life and godliness, through the true knowledge of Him who called us by His own glory and excellence. ⁴ For by these He has granted to us His precious and magnificent promises, so that by them you may become partakers of *the* divine nature, having escaped the corruption that is in the world by lust.⁵ Now for this very reason also, applying all diligence, in your faith supply moral excellence, and in *your* moral excellence, knowledge,⁶ and in *your* knowledge, self-control, and in *your* self-control, perseverance, and in *your* perseverance, godliness,⁷ and in *your* godliness, brotherly kindness, and in *your* brotherly kindness, love. ⁸ For if these *qualities* are yours and are increasing, they render you neither useless nor unfruitful in the true knowledge of our Lord Jesus Christ. ⁹ For he who lacks these *qualities* is blind *or* short-sighted, having forgotten *his* purification from his former sins.¹⁰

Therefore, brethren, be all the more diligent to make certain about His calling and choosing you; for as long as you practice these things, you will never stumble; [11] for in this way the entrance into the eternal kingdom of our Lord and Savior Jesus Christ will be abundantly supplied to you.

[12] Therefore, I will always be ready to remind you of these things, even though you *already* know *them*, and have been established in the truth which is present with *you*. [13] I consider it right, as long as I am in this *earthly* dwelling, to stir you up by way of reminder, [14] knowing that the laying aside of my *earthly* dwelling is imminent, as also our Lord Jesus Christ has made clear to me. [15] And I will also be diligent that at any time after my departure you will be able to call these things to mind.[15]

As I have spoken about the spiritual disciplines among faith leaders, I've heard, "Yeah, but...," more times than I can number. At a leadership conference I referenced the hundreds of biblical imperatives to action. A long-time pastor replied, "Yeah, but those are all plural statements." I confess: I don't have the faintest idea why singular or plural is relevant to the argument and I was so stunned by his dismissal of Scripture I didn't have a reply, but his point was clear: Those imperatives don't apply. He dismissed as not applicable perhaps one-and-a-half thousand imperatives—from just the New Testament— because they are written in the plural form (?)! Another man, a nationally-known speaker, waved his hand dismissively at the subject of the disciplines throughout church history—and with his wave dismissed two-thousand years of church history as "...not truly understanding the message of God's grace and justification." Once again, I was speechless.

---

[15] 2 Peter 1:1-15.

What's driving this resistance to practicing the disciplines of faith while proclaiming devotion to grace?

I have no intention of being harsh in these pages, but neither do I intend to let us off the hook. There is no consistency of faith without consistent practice of the faith's disciplines. And my, my, my. Has there ever been a better time than now for faith to wield a sharp edge, shine a bright light, inspire thirst for the Gospel, and provide anchorage for our souls?

The pursuit of any discipline requires practice and all of life is a discipline, including the spiritual life. Fail to discipline yourself, and no matter your earthly endeavor, you will fail. Yes, you are the recipient and beneficiary of the finished and completed work of Jesus Christ on your behalf. But it is not only imperative that you believe this is true, it is imperative that you are able to implement the truth into daily living lest your faith be useless to you this side of the pearly gates. There can be no consistent implementation without consistent practice of the spiritual disciplines, the same disciplines demonstrated and employed by Jesus Christ during His tenure on earth.

Whether you are learning to play a musical instrument, swing a golf club, kick a ball, cast a fly, cook a tenderloin, make a pie, or write computer code, each requires repetitive effort that is evaluated, critiqued, and practiced again, and again, and again if you hope to master the discipline.

Implied in this repetitive effort is failure—not the failure of not showing up and trying, but the inherent failure that comes with learning mastery of a complex system. Nothing that matters is mastered without repeated effort and repeated failure. Mastery comes from successive approximation—repetitive effort that develops and sophisticates a skill necessary to the discipline you are seeking to master.

Evaluation. Measurement. Critique. Repetition. Development. These are essential tools within discipline.

In the pages that follow, you will read a recurring disclaimer, a statement of clarification, intended to remind you what exactly you are developing. The practice of the spiritual disciplines is likely the most abused, misrepresented fundamental of the Christian life. It's not uncommon for biblical teachers to attach your personal acceptance to your ability to perform the primary elements of the Christian life.

Personal acceptance? That's right. Your spiritual wellbeing and standing with yourself, others, and God is often attached to your ability to look right, act right, walk right, do right. Fail in your Christian performance, and your acceptance proves tenuous—with your critics, and by implication, with God too.

While performance is important,[16] it has nothing to do with your personal acceptance with God. As far as your heavenly Father is concerned, you are accepted singularly on the basis of what you have done with Jesus Christ. If you have asked Him into your life to reign, rule, and live through you, God says you are accepted. Absolutely. Perfectly. Irrevocably. If you have not invited Christ into your life as your Savior and Lord, the One who justifies you with God, then you are outside of Christ and apart from God.

Acceptance with God is binary: You are either in Christ and accepted or you are outside of Christ and distant from God.

We will explore this in greater depth as we go, but the point for now is that since your acceptance with God has nothing to do with your performance, *you are free to practice* your performance without risking rejection. As we will see, in your heart-of-hearts—the deepest aspect of your being—you desire to know God, walk with Him, and understand His ways.

---

[16] Cf.: Ephesians 2:10; Titus 2:14.

Practicing the disciplines of the faith are the keys to realizing your heart's desire.

At a basic level, if you are a Christian then your future is secured. Through the sacrificial effort of Jesus Christ, your sinfulness and sins are forgiven. You are made new, and when you die, heaven is your destiny. You are free to do nothing more with your faith.

The problem is, your heart desires more than forgiveness and heaven when you die. Further, life on this orb is a raucous, careening, irregular, asymmetrical dance with the devil. The primary message of God to you is that He is present, He understands what's at stake, and He is pledged to meet each day and every aspect of life from within you and through you. You are not on your own and you are not alone—unless you prefer it that way.

By definition, the disciplines of the faith are those places where you meet with God and He meets with you. Your heart desires to know God, and by practicing the spiritual disciplines, your heart finds satisfaction.

It's true: Salvation is through Christ alone, by faith alone. As Ephesians says, "For by grace you have been saved through faith; and that not of yourselves, it is the gift of God; not as a result of works, that no one should boast."[17] The point is: You can't save yourself. Salvation and right-standing with God are a gift from God through Christ. Further: There is nothing that you can do to improve, maintain, advance, or more firmly establish your standing with God. If there was, then the "finished" work of Christ wouldn't be finished and salvation wouldn't be a gift.

While most conservative theologians believe the above paragraph, in their quest to inspire you to act like a Christian, some tie sanctification to your ability to perform. By

---

[17] Ephesians 2:8-9.

sanctification, I mean your acceptance and secure standing with God. So while saying one thing about the finished work of Christ, it's not uncommon to be taught that you are saved by grace and perfected—sanctified—by how well you perform.

In addition to being poor theology, this performance-based acceptance applies tremendous pressure on you to get it right lest you create a barrier between you and God. After all, who wants to be on the outs with God?

But while this teaching is common, it is unbiblical and incorrect. It has to be! You can't have the biblical books of Hebrews, Romans, Galatians, Ephesians, et al declaring that Jesus Christ removed all the barriers that stand between you and God only to then declare that He didn't actually remove *all* the barriers.

Jesus Christ either satisfied God's just requirements or He didn't.

Thus, there is nothing you can do to cause God to love and accept you more than He already does if you are in Christ Jesus. Conversely, there is nothing you can *fail to do* that will cause God to accept and love you less than He already does if you are in Christ Jesus.

You are accepted.

Therefore, you are totally free, and freely responsible, without substantive risk, to pursue your heart's desire of knowing God and walking with Him. Your journey will not be without stumbles, weaving, and an occasional run-off into the ditch. Such is life. But in your determined trust of reliance upon the Spirit of God there is also copious mercy given through Christ.

God doesn't expect you to get life perfectly right. He does expect you to show up, engage with Him, and learn His ways. Isn't this true of all vibrant relationships? You both show up and bring everything you've got to the relationship.

Given this, it's essential to understand that a relationship is undergirded with disciplines, even your relationship with God—disciplines not unlike playing the piano, for example.

A pianist doesn't practice by repetitively attempting to play Rachmaninoff's Piano Sonata number 2 in B-flat minor. Rather, a serious student of the piano prepares to play Rachmaninoff by practicing the scales, proper finger placement, mental attitude, and preparatory pieces. In order to play Rachmaninoff well, mastery of the fundamental disciplines for playing the piano are essential.

Pianists consider the above piece by Rachmaninoff the most intense of his compositions. Unless a pianist is disciplined to endure the intensity this piece demands, they will fail at the endeavor of playing Rachmaninoff.

Life. Life is intense. The basic lesson we learn as we mature is that life gets more demanding, not less. That's the bad news. The good news is that as a Christian you are indwelt by the Holy Spirit of God. His job is to come alongside you, encourage you, explain God (Himself) to you, and guide you into all manner of truth.

So, like I said: You are not alone and you are not on your own. Trusting and calling upon the Spirit to live through you is what the Bible calls walking in the Spirit. Determining to approach life independently of the Spirit is what the Bible calls walking after the flesh. How you approach daily living is your choice, but in full disclosure, the Bible says that this choice is actually a spiritual war, an intense conflict, and it exhorts you repeatedly to prepare for this lifelong struggle.[18]

Now we are back to an earlier point: As a secure person who is irrevocably included in the life of Christ, your heart desires to know God and God wants to meet you and live through you in

[18] Cf.: Galatians 5.

the bumps and grind of life. In fact, Scripture notes that Jesus Christ suffered in every way you do during His tenure on earth just so He could honestly say to you, "I understand."[19]

Comprehending and implementing the above paragraph is realized by disciplining yourself in the spiritual practices, the fundamentals of the faith. Your relationship with God is not improved by practicing the spiritual disciplines, but it is enlightened. And, your ability to walk in the Spirit and resist the attacks of the enemy is sophisticated by practicing the spiritual fundamentals.[20]

---

[19] Cf.: Hebrew 4:15.
[20] Cf.: Romans 12:1-2; Hebrews 5:14.

Questions and Considerations

1. The lament Paul writes about in Romans 7:14 ff—"For what I am doing, I do not understand; for I am not practicing what I would like to do, but I am doing the very thing I hate"—is the deep-seated dissatisfaction of inconsistency. He desires to do one thing, but then does something contrary. As Paul continues writing, he presents what is true for Believers and in 8:5 introduces the concept of mental focus, i.e., setting your mind on truth. The idea of "setting" implies a consistency of determination, thought, and action. But where does this consistency come from? How is it created? Jim Collins is quoted at the front of *Rigorous Grace* saying, "Discipline is consistency of action." If discipline is key to consistency, and if your desire as a Christian is consistency of thought and action with what is true, what is the push-back, even the revulsion, to discipline in your Christian life and walk?

2. The Bible speaks of grace and mercy. It speaks of walking in the power of the Holy Spirit, trusting Christ who is your life to live His life—the Christian life—through you. But Scripture also speaks of discipline, faith in action, a determined perseverance to bring all that you have to bear on all that life brings your way. What makes grace, mercy, walking in the Spirit, and trusting Christ compatible and complimentary with

spiritual discipline? Or not? Some insist discipline is legalistic, and therefore incompatible with freedom and grace in Christ. Agree or disagree? Why?

3. From the earliest pages of Scripture, there is the battle between good and evil with humankind caught in between these opposing forces. It is the battle between dark and light, your way versus God's, flesh versus spirit. What is your understanding of walking after the flesh versus walking in the Spirit and why is this important to realizing your heart's desire?

TWO

Habits and Learning

Practice is essential to improve your understanding and performance. This is true for all aspects of substantive effort, including your ability, skill, understanding, and knowledge of your spiritual life.

Still though, what do practice and discipline look like and entail? Yes, there is repetition, evaluation, measurement, failure and success. But why? To what end? What exactly are you developing within your soul?

At a high level, practicing a discipline builds a habit. Habits can be simple or complex.

You have a habit for brushing your teeth, using a fork, driving a car, and riding a bicycle. For the most part, these are simple habits in that you can perform the basics without thinking about them.

Complex habits span the spectrum of your soul. So, reading a book for comprehension, negotiating plans with your spouse, crafting a new initiative at work, or nurturing a relationship each tend toward complexity. Complex habits are the complex patterns you have for thinking (mind), feeling (emotion), and behaving (will). But it's not just that complex habits guide you through complex tasks, complex habits maintain and facilitate your confidence and abilities during times of duress.

Craig Weller and Jonathan Pope are the Founders of Building the Elite,[21] a training program for people aspiring to selection by the military special forces. Not that this is our aspiration, but these two guys have incredible insight into the rationale underlying discipline and the associated practices.

I was surprised to realize that the majority—60%-90%—of folks who washout of the grueling special forces training do so because they fail mentally, *not* physically. Not only did this surprise me, but I find this applicable to why you and I are considering discipline. We're not likely to need to master close-quarters combat, underwater demolition, and running uphill for twenty miles carrying a pack... but in the training trials of life how many folks do you know who've failed in their faith, or who feel their faith in Christ has failed them, especially when facing stress, duress, and disillusionment? Why did they fail?

The Bible wouldn't tell you to "set your mind" if a significant aspect of daily faith and practice were not mental—and it tells you to do this over and over.

Weller and Pope report:

> A study on causes of attrition in Special Operations Forces (SOF) selection (in this case, BUD/S students)

---

[21] Cf.: *BuildingTheElite.com*.

found that <u>80% of those who left the course did so voluntarily. They quit.</u>

Just 10% were medically dropped due to injuries.

Only about 6-7% were dropped for performance failures, and the rest were separated for various administrative reasons.

This is important. Anywhere from roughly 60-90% of those who begin these courses will not make it through to the other side, but most of them are not physically broken when they drop. They're often not even below performance standards. They just choose to leave.

These environments are designed to be as discouraging as possible. They [the trainers] want to get students to a place in which every possible external factor is discouraging - telling them that they don't have what it takes, that they're not good enough, that it's not worth trying.

They want to see what happens when the only thing telling students that they have what it takes to keep going is the voice in their own heads. They're evaluating for internal drive under conditions of extreme stress and external negative feedback.[22]

I'm struck by two lines in particular: a) "These [training] environments are designed to be as discouraging as possible," and b) the trainers are isolating "the voice in their [the student's] own heads" to evaluate internal drive under stress and negative feedback.

---

[22] Cf.: Weller, Craig and Pope, Jonathan. *Instagram.com/BuildingTheElite.*

NEVER SURRENDER...
NEVER GIVE UP!

Not that life is a total beat-down, but there are many times when discouragement far outpaces encouragement. While victory is yours in Christ, your experience of victory during times of discouragement, and your ability to stay focused when victory seems fantastical, is directly correlated to your ability to hear the voice of the Holy Spirit in your head.

Over and over in their writing, Weller and Pope isolate the critical importance of building mental and emotional habits to manage intense training. Said another way, physical training and the associated habits is not nearly as critical as is your mental-emotional ability to habitually regulate and manage stress.

Like I said, this isn't a book about preparing you to be a military special operator. This is a book written to prepare you to live spiritually as your heart desires and walk with God as He designed and equipped you to do throughout all your days, all your ways, and in spite of whatever discouragement and duress you encounter.

The Bible has things to say about your physical wellbeing and preparation to live a healthy life. But much more common in Scripture is exhortation for how to prepare your mind as a Believer. "Set your mind," Paul writes. "Practice," he says in Philippians. "Train yourself for godliness," he writes to Timothy. "Practice" to discern, Hebrews says.[23]

In short, a similar washout rate applies to life as applies to special operations training. Life is primarily a mind game. Knowing God is a desire of the heart. Passion fuels each. Discipline and the practice to habituate it develops those patterns that guide your walk with Christ and create resiliency in life.

---

[23] Colossians 3:2; Philippians 4:8-9; 1 Timothy 4:7; Hebrews 5:12.

I've mentioned failure a couple of times in this chapter. In his book about learning, David Epstein[24] discovered that in order to learn deeply, failure is essential. What Epstein means by deep learning is contrasted against regular learning. Deep learning is resilient and flexible, he says. By resilient he means learning that doesn't wither, waffle, or falter when under duress. By flexible, he means learning with sufficient insight and mastery that you can apply what you've learned in various and unrelated environments. But you don't get deep learning without suffering failure.

Is this registering for you? Are you correlating this yet to your faith and life?

Recall that Jesus Christ, even though He was God's Son, "learned obedience from the things which He suffered."[25] And wow! Was it ever important that Jesus had a deep learning of obedience and understanding about His Father, God. What would have happened—to you, to me, to us—if Jesus' obedience had failed in the Garden of Gethsemane?

The goal of the Christian life, at least as far as your heavenly Father is concerned, is not to get it right but to learn His ways and who He is. You have been made right by your redemption and sanctification in Christ. What you may not possess, however, is the deep learning that can be yours as a disciple of Jesus Christ.

To be clear, I'm not talking about the kinds of things you learn from a sermon or by reading a book. I'm talking about learning that is honed and developed through the stress and failures you suffer in life throughout your days. When life takes an irregular turn, the inevitable accusation Satan makes is that God has abandoned you, is not doing right by you, or that your faith is irrelevant to the situation causing you angst. It is essential that

---

[24] Epstein, David. *Range*. Riverhead Books. New York, NY. 2019.
[25] Cf.: Hebrews 5:8.

you learn deeply who God is, who you are, and how your relationship works. Although you may pray for deliverance—and God certainly hears your prayer—routine rescue as a remedy for hardship is the worst thing God could do for you. You will never learn God's ways and construct an enduring faith apart from struggle.

In studying deep learning, Robin Hogarth identified two environments in which learning occurs: "kind" and "wicked."[26]

A kind environment is one where patterns repeat and feedback is accurate and rapid. A wicked environment is one in which the rules of the game are not clear or are incomplete, there may or may not be repeating patterns, and they may or may not be obvious. Feedback is often delayed, inaccurate, or both. It's not uncommon in some wicked learning environments for experience to reinforce the exact wrong lessons.

Now, think about your life. Think about raising your kids, managing illness, aging parents, the insurance company that won't pay, the financial loss, the irregularity of our national schisms, what your kids are learning in school, soaring crime rates.... You do not live in a kind environment.

Life is a wicked environment.

What are you learning? How are you learning? What are you developing, changing, modifying in order to bring your faith to bear upon the wicked environment in which you live?

When the Bible speaks about "disciplining yourself," it's not necessarily exhorting you to acquire more biblical insight. Certainly biblical content and information are important, but unless what you conceptually know is tempered into deep learning, there is a high probability that in the wicked environment of life your faith may be found lacking in power,

---

[26] Hogarth, Robin. *Educating Intuition*. University of Chicago Press. Chicago, IL. 2001.

relevance, or applicability when the inevitable demands of this life close in around you. In a wicked environment, a kind faith is vulnerable to a God who is accused of being distant, disengaged, irrelevant, or even petty and capricious.

But in contrast, in a wicked environment where your faith is forged into deep learning, you and your walk of faith prove not only resilient and flexible as Epstein discovered, you are also powerful and threatening to the dark kingdom and its minions. Oorah! I just heard Cash growling in my head, "Stand me up at the gates of hell, but I won't back down."

Learning forms habits and habits reinforce learning—it's a compounding dynamic. As you read, and ponder, and seek to apply the practices that follow, I encourage you to pray and ask your heavenly Father to show you whose you are, what you believe, what your habits are, and where change needs to begin in order to realize your heart's desire. The top priority in God's list of pressing matters is His relationship with you and yours with Him. Everything else pales in comparison to His future with you. This means that when you pray the prayer I'm suggesting, God leaps to answer and take you at your word. So, speak with your heavenly Father about the practices that follow.

There are several definitions for the word "discipline" in the dictionary. One of those is punitive, meaning: Discipline occurs when you do something wrong and discomfort is introduced designed to make you behave correctly next time in order to avoid further discomfort. As a kid growing up, if I was late getting home, Mom disciplined me by forbidding me to play with my buddies for a few days. The pain of not getting to be with my friends motivated me to not be late getting home once I regained my freedom of movement.

But discipline is much more elegant than the above paragraph alone conveys. Discipline encompasses order, training,

development, expertise in a given endeavor; it is the means to building character, honor, respect, consistency, reliability, exemplary conduct, dependable patterning and behavior, integrity, and constancy; discipline exists hand-in-hand with groundedness, perseverance, determination, grit, preparation, and informed conviction; it is systematic, routine, procedural, and freeing. Discipline creates self-control. Discipline makes you free. HONESTY – HONOR – CIVILITY
Discipline places you in position to be all that you are destined to be, but discipline requires practice.

Yes, discipline has a punitive component to it. But I trust the strings of your heart are resonating with the vision I just cast of discipline's scope. Discipline is expansive, visionary, compelling, and coercive. Reconsider the previous paragraph and apply each aspect of discipline to the concept of your spiritual faith.

An astounding passage of Scripture is recorded in the Book of John.[27] In it, Jesus repeatedly challenges the staid and stolid status quo with the promise of freedom for those who know Him. "You shall know the truth and the truth shall set you free," He told them. The passage concludes when the staid and stolid pick up stones to throw at Jesus in order to destroy the freedom challenging their stability in the status quo.

Freedom was so powerful, so magnificent, and so challenging that it nearly cost Jesus His life in John 8. Ultimately, eleven chapters later, John reports that the cost of freedom was indeed Jesus' life: death by crucifixion. Freedom is powerful, and just as Aristotle said, "Through discipline comes freedom."

My critics disparage my views in this book. They insist we are free from discipline because we are made right with God through Jesus Christ. And, they are correct—sort of: We are

---

[27] Cf.: John 8, esp. v. 32.

made right—justified—with God through Christ. But their critique is shortsighted and it shortchanges the accomplishments of Christ. Yes, we are made right... but what remains is believing with enough substantive conviction and habitual skill to implement, sophisticate, and understand what theological justification means and how this guides our thinking, emotion, and behavior.

Jesus Christ came to live in you in order to live His life through you. Christianity is not simply forgiveness of your sins and heaven when you die. Christianity is the incarnation of Jesus Christ through you into a world in desperate need of hope. Christianity is the invasion of Christ into the dark domain of Satan's lair. You are a soldier of light, a bearer of Good News, a representative of the Kingdom of God, and you are endowed with the unconditional love of God to dispense into the toxic environment of men and women, boys and girls, laboring in the degradation of this fallen world. Within each soul is the God-shaped vacuum that lusts for a new and better way, something more magnificent than the stumbling, stubbing, lurching effort to earn the favor of others and a distant deity through performance and sacrifice. A freedom bearer in this environment cannot reasonably expect to carry the torch of Christianity without a resilient, flexible, and dynamic faith honed to readiness through practiced discipline.

If you desire for your faith to work day in, day out, it is not good enough to believe God. Recall: Scripture states that the demons believe, and do so with such conviction that they tremble.[28] For your belief to do you any earthly good, it must be applied in such a way that it works within a wicked environment with enough sophistication to be both resilient and flexible. The only way to realize this aspiration is through practice of each discipline of the faith.

---

[28] Cf.: James 2:19.

Weller and Pope again:

> Remember that performance is not practice. We want to perform automatically, but practice intentionally.
>
> Experts practice by finding ways to avoid automated behavior and stay focused with top-down conscious attention.
>
> Only through this deliberate focus can we learn new things and change our subconscious behaviors.
>
> Our brains are neuroplastic: They can rewire and adapt to new ways of thinking, moving, and being—but this process only happens with attention.[29]

Unless you are a critic, you have picked up this book because you desire to know your heavenly Father better. You desire to walk with Him more closely, and more than anything, you desire to *know Him* not just know *about* Him. Good for you! You are following your heart's desire.

Don't overthink discipline. Above all, don't be so narrowminded as to only define discipline as punitive or punishing. It is these when applicable, but it is also training, correcting, enlightening, pursuing deep understanding, making applicable, perfecting, instructing, guiding, developing, growing, sophisticating, executing reliably, exercising self-control, building character, ordering your conduct, developing a systematic and reliable faith, coming to truly know, developing a close affinity, and trusting without succumbing to doubt.

In short, when you associate the characteristics in the previous paragraph with your walk of faith and your experience of coming to know your heavenly Father better, you have a robust

---

[29] Weller and Pope. Ibid.

definition of what it means to be a disciple of Jesus Christ—and note: disciple and discipline enjoy the same root word.

When applied to your faith, practicing the disciplines of the Christian life are the keys to knowing God, understanding how He thinks, grasping His action in your life, and seizing upon your desire to align your thought, emotion, and behavior with what is true of you, true of your life in Christ, and all that is representative of your place in God's family and Kingdom. As you practice, just as Scripture promises, you will be transformed by the renewing of your mind.[30] Meaning: You will increase and sophisticate your ability to practically demonstrate what is true, problem-solve when you fall short, and progressively comprehend your heavenly Father's thought, character, motive, and manner.

All that remains is getting on with it.

As Hebrews 12 begins, the author takes us to the ramparts of heaven and portrays a raucous, roaring crowd, on their feet cheering, screaming, and exhorting. Who are these unruly fans? They are the millions of saints who have preceded you in life. Each one of these who are loosened from earth's bonds now sees clearly: God is indeed absolutely good. Jesus Christ is everything attributed to Him. The Spirit is in fact the roaring furnace of God's love and abiding presence. Faith is now without doubt and trust is absolutely justified.

Even though your face is dust-caked, your head bloodied, and your body aching from the duress of life's arena, can you hear them screaming your name? Can you hear their exhortation?

"Advance, brother!"

"Seize the moment, sister!"

GOD IS GOOD ALL THE TIME AND ALL THE TIME GOD IS GOOD.

---

[30] Cf.: Romans 12:1-2.

"Stay with it. Keep on! Forge ahead. All that you believe is true."

"Keep your wits about you!"

Quoting now from Hebrews:

> Do you see what this means—all these pioneers who blazed the way, all these veterans cheering us on? It means we'd better get on with it. Strip down, start running—and never quit! No extra spiritual fat, no parasitic sins. Keep your eyes on Jesus, who both began and finished this race we're in. Study how he did it. Because he never lost sight of where he was headed— that exhilarating finish in and with God—he could put up with anything along the way: Cross, shame, whatever. And now he's *there*, in the place of honor, right alongside God. When you find yourselves flagging in your faith, go over that story again, item by item, that long litany of hostility he plowed through. *That* will shoot adrenaline into your souls![31]

---

[31] Hebrews 12:1-3, *The Message*.

Questions and Considerations

1. Chapter 2 presents a strong correlation between the mental discipline of military training and the mental discipline described in Scripture. Is the correlation legitimate, illegitimate, over-stated, or accurate to the point of being applicable to your Christian life? How does your answer to this question guide your spiritual life moving forward?

2. The researcher Robin Hogarth identifies two arenas in which learning occurs: kind environments and wicked environments. Are there kind environments in your life? Are there wicked environments? Given your answer, what can you expect to learn, and to what extent, in your life's learning environments and how does this correlate to your spiritual life?

3. This chapter asserts that the desire of your heart is to know God and walk with Him. Agree or disagree? Why? Assuming the assertion of this chapter is correct and is aligned with Scripture's presentation of your true heart's desire, how will your heart's desire be realized and at what cost?

THREE

The Life of Faith

"

"The sin of respectable people reveals itself in flight from responsibility."

John W. Doberstein

Faith. Performance. Independent of each other? Co-dependent? Or, something else?

The Catholic-monk-reformer Martin Luther (1483-1546), was tremendously frustrated with his inability to live a godly enough life to justify God's forgiveness and acceptance of him into heaven. At the peak of his disillusionment, he encountered Romans 1:17, "The righteous man, shall live, by faith."

Faith, period.

Faith, alone.

Luther studied. He enhanced his ability to read the original language of the New Testament. He argued that the force of the context surrounding Romans 1:17 merited a translation that added "alone" to the end of the sentence: "The righteous man, shall live, by faith. Alone."

Before his life was over, Luther would nearly pay with his life for his embrace of this biblical passage.

Luther appropriated scriptural truth into his life and discovered the true Gospel. The works-based salvation he adopted and practiced as a monk was bankrupted and his discovery of salvation by faith alone, in Christ alone, launched the Protestant Reformation.

But Protestants, like Catholics, struggled to believe that acceptance with God did not require human contribution. Consequently, while holding theologically to *sola Christos* and *sola fide*—salvation by *Christ alone* through *faith alone*—practical acceptance with God returned to being conditional, a performance-based acceptance: You are saved by grace, but you are perfected and accepted by God through performance.

As incredulous as it seems, Scripture is clear: God does not relate to you on a performance-based acceptance. Rather, He justifies and sanctifies you—accepts you and sets you apart as His child—on a Jesus-based acceptance. This is the sole basis He uses to justify your existence.

I like these lines from Paul David Tripp:

> No one who really understands what Scripture has to say about the comprehensive, every-aspect-of-your-personhood-altering nature of sin would ever think that anyone could muster enough motivation and strength to rise to God's standard of perfection. The

thought that any fallen human being would be able to perform his or her way into acceptance with God has to be the most insane of all delusions.[32]

Not only salvation, but justification, redemption, sanctification, and acceptance with God must be through Christ alone, by faith alone. If you have declared Jesus Christ the Lord of your life and invited Him to reign in your heart, then you are in Christ, a recipient of His life, and you are completely accepted by God. If not, you are not accepted by God.[33]

Said another way, if you are in Christ there is nothing you can do to cause God to accept you more than He already does. The converse is true as well: There is nothing you can do to cause God to accept you less than He does if you are in Christ.

However, Paul states that God created us for good works and intends for us to perform accordingly.[34] James declares that faith without accompanying performance is dead.[35] Titus notes that we who are the possession of God are "zealous for good deeds."[36] The biblical books of Philippians, Hebrews, Peter, John, and Revelation each exhort us to "practice" righteousness.[37] Paul instructs Timothy to guide his church's implementation of their faith: "Instruct them [his congregants] to do good, to be rich in

---

[32] Tripp, Paul David. *New Morning Mercies: A Daily Gospel Devotional*. Crossway. Wheaton, IL. 2014.

[33] To know more about becoming a Christian, one who follows Jesus Christ and enjoys eternal life with Him, reference the Appendices for "How to Become a Christian.".

[34] Cf.: Ephesians 2:10 and the broader context of 2:4-10.

[35] Cf.: James 2:17 and the broader context of James' argument in 2:14-26.

[36] Cf.: Titus 2:14.

[37] Cf.: Philippians 4:9; Hebrews 5:14; 2 Peter 1:10; 1 John 3:7ff; Revelation 22:11.

good works, to be generous and ready to share."[38] The letter to the Corinthians simply tells us to "do what is right"[39] and John says, "Little children, let us not love with word or with tongue, but in deed and truth."[40] My Dad used to say, "God is very interested in your performance. What you do is important. It just doesn't have anything to do with your acceptance."

Thus, performance is established as important to God but is taken out of the salvation and acceptance equation. *Sola Christos, sola fide.* Given the transformation of this great grace portrayed in the Gospel, you may concur with Paul that you are created in Christ for good works.

Faith and works are connected—even reflective of each other, as James writes[41]—yet they remain independent.

Why?

Your salvation, the acceptance it gains you with God, and your establishment as a member of God's family is very problematic for Satan, the dark lord of this world. Once you are born again, you are secured—sealed[42]—in Christ by the Holy Spirit.[43] This establishment is part of an irrevocable trust—a covenant or testament—between the Trinity. Not

---

[38] 1 Timothy 6:18 (17-19). Note: Paul's direct counsel is toward those who are "rich in this present world." Certainly this is wise counsel to those who are monetarily established, but once we grasp the riches that are ours in Christ Jesus (cf.: Eph. 2:7; Phil. 4:19; Col. 1:27), can there be any doubt the counsel of 1 Tm. 6:18 applies just as well to the church regardless of our bank accounts?
[39] Cf.: 2 Corinthians 13:7.
[40] 1 John 3:18.
[41] Cf.: James 2:18.
[42] Cf.: 2 Corinthians 1:22.
[43] Cf.: Ephesians 1:13.

only is your salvation irrevocable, it is unchangeable, and it exists in perpetuity.[44]

For you, this is Good News. But for Satan, this is really bad news.

As Satan grapples with the grace of God to save and transform fallen humankind, the best he can do is bend orthodox theology to create heresy. He reasons, *The people of God are included in the life of Christ, but if I can tempt them to associate their effort as a contributing force in their salvation, then the magnificence of salvation by faith in Christ alone will be marginalized in their lives, attitudes, and actions.*

Thus, your salvation is established, but out of the dark desperation in which Satan languishes there are deceptions designed to pervert the grace of God and the completed work of Jesus Christ. As you walk with Christ, on either side of the path of faith there are precipices. A misstep means a departure and fall away from the truth of grace into the deception of performance-based acceptance or rejection.

On one side there is the chasm of legalism, performance-based acceptance. The thought is, *God will love me more, accept me more, be more pleased with me, etc. if I perform well.*

On the other side of the walk of faith, there is the valley of license: *Since I'm saved and secured in Christ, totally and*

---

[44] To understand this trust between the Trinity, I recommend Malcolm Smith's book, *The Power of the Blood Covenant*. Harrison House Inc. Tulsa, OK. 2002.

completely forgiven, why not live like hell in this life and still enjoy heaven when I die?

Spiritual performance because God expects it of you is a derivation of *legalism*. But passivity about performance, or indifference to it, is a derivation of *license*.

Martin Luther was not a fan of the Book of James. But James' book remains one of the inspired books of the Bible. As much as Luther struggled with it, and as tempting as it is to over-embrace or under-embrace his writing, James' spiritual reasoning still stands: "You have faith and I have works; show me your faith without the works, and I will show you my faith by my works."[45]

Faith alone. *Sola fide*. Certainly!

Yet, the other side of the argument is also valid and biblical. You are created for good works[46]— "zealous for good deeds," as is written in Titus.[47]

Acceptance with God is established by faith in Christ alone. This set Martin Luther free from his works-based salvation. Yet he, like you and me, had to live. Thus, he said, "God does not need my good works, but my neighbor does." In another place, "If you want to change the world, pick up your pen and write." And as well, "I don't always nail things to church doors, but when I do stuff happens."

The final quote might have come from the left field of my brain, but the others are Martin himself. In them you can hear him aligning his faith and his performance while leaving his salvation established. As much as he disliked

---

[45] James 2:18.
[46] Cf.: Ephesians 2:10.
[47] Cf.: Titus 2:14.

James, as he digested that he was righteous by faith (Romans 1:17), he eventually connected behavior to belief (James 2:18). Romans 5-8 and Ephesians 2:8-9 are not in conflict with the Book of James, and neither is Romans 1:17, the verse that transformed Luther's theology and life.

Your new person, called elsewhere a new creation,[48] is transformed from darkness to light. Upon salvation, you are accepted, secured, justified, and endowed with a new heart. This new heart is the seat of the indwelling Christ, the place of the Holy Spirit. On its walls are inscribed the dreams and desires of God.[49]

Thus, when you live truly from your heart, you exhibit behavior reflective of God and representative of your true self. In Christ alone, by faith alone, you are saved and secured and transformed. When apprehended, taken aboard, grasped, embraced, your behavior reflects and is representative of your heavenly Father and your new person. This is what the Bible means when it says that you walk by faith.[50]

Performance makes faith objective. By this I mean: Observing, wrestling, and wrangling with your behavior to make it correlate with your theological belief moves your faith from the realm of theological subjectivity to the realm of your objective, experiential reality.

You may ponder, *What does it mean to have faith?*

---

[48] Cf.: 2 Corinthians 5:17.

[49] Cf.: the prophesies of Ezekiel 36:26 and Jeremiah 31:33, also quoted in Hebrews 8:7-13. To read more about your new identity in Christ: Gillham, Bill. *Lifetime Guarantee.* Harvest House Publishers. Eugene, OR. 1993.

[50] Cf.: 2 Corinthians 5:7.

Your performance is a demonstration of your belief. Performance makes your faith objective—objective in the sense that you can evaluate your actual belief by observing how you perform. If your performance does not match your heart's true desire and orthodox theology, you are able to make adjustments so that your faith and your works align.

Said another way, performance can either represent or misrepresent faith. In Christ, by faith, you are established. When your performance is contrary to your true self, the incongruity serves you by contrasting God's truth against your performance. When incongruity occurs, the Bible calls it sin, falling short, or walking after the flesh.

Your standard, your fixed point from which you navigate life is absolute, unflinching confidence in the finished work of Jesus Christ on your behalf. This standard is the singular factor in your justification, sanctification, acceptance, redemption, and transformation. Against this fixed point you evaluate and benefit from your performance in order to make the abstraction of grace concrete understanding, knowledge, and wisdom. While you are transformed and made new, this is the rationale by which you experience transformation. As you implement, you demonstrate your faith by your performance/works.

What's the point?

The point is, this new heart you possess as a new person in Christ desires to please God,[51] not to gain greater acceptance—an impossibility—but because it is the impetus that drives your new heart. Thus, true faith is faith

---

[51] Ruth Haley Barton writes, "You may not realize it, but your desire for God is the truest and most essential thing about you. Your desire for God and your capacity to connect with God as a human soul is the essence of who you are." Ref. Barton, Ruth Haley. *Invitation to Solitude and Silence.* IVP Books. Downers Grove, IL. 2010.

that performs, not to gain or enhance salvation or standing with God, but because it is in your heart to perform in keeping with your transformed person.

Faith is abstract. Performance is objective—serving you either positively or negatively to better understand God and yourself. Practiced disciplines in your life are the control factors that enable you to assess, evaluate, measure, and modify your spiritual skill—your ability to consistently execute what is in your heart to do—while living life.

This conflict, tension, and laboring to demonstrate faith through works is nothing new. A disciplined spiritual life has been practiced for centuries. What the Gospel establishes for the disciplined spiritual life is that rigorous, spiritual discipline is not done to gain God's favor but is motivated to demonstrate your heart that is made new, your soul that is secured, and your life that is guided by the indwelling Holy Spirit.

In your heart, you desire to know more about who God is and who you are. The most effective way to realize this desire is via spiritual discipline. In fact, from the biblical writers until now, a set of disciplines have emerged that are simply called, the spiritual disciplines.

Referencing back to the walk of faith having precipices on either side of the path, Richard Foster defines the path itself: "The spiritual disciplines are like a narrow ridge with a sheer drop-off on either side: there is the abyss of trust in works on one side and the abyss of faith without deeds on the other. On the ridge there is a path, the disciplines of the spiritual life. The path does not produce change; it only places us where the change can occur."[52]

A change in what?

You have been changed, made new. You are set apart for God and to God—what the Bible calls being sanctified.[53] This relationship, or juxtaposition, that you have with God was established at the moment of your salvation. This is the truth that rocked Martin Luther's world and theology.

Christ alone, by faith alone. In a word: grace. Quoting Ephesians again, "For by grace you have been saved through faith; and that not of yourselves, it is the gift of God; not as a result of works, that no one should boast."[54]

Yet, you labor to live truly and truly live. You struggle to reflect in your behavior what is true of yourself and God. You are motivated to refine your understanding, to see more clearly, and to perform more accurately and compellingly the truth of your true desires.

Practicing the rigor of the spiritual disciplines puts you in position to encounter God and experience *change* in how you live, perform, behave, and think. Yes, you are sanctified, but as you walk the path of faith and practice the spiritual disciplines, your experience of sanctification is enlightened. You change, grow, develop, sophisticate; your behavioral consistency improves and this renders spiritual satisfaction and confidence. Your faith is informed, your trust is increased, and your understanding of God—your knowing

---

[52] Richard Foster. *Celebration of Discipline*. Hodder and Stoughton. London, England. 2008.
[53] Cf.: 1 Corinthians 6:11.
[54] Ephesians 2:8-9.

of Him—is enhanced because you have encountered Him. Thus, His presence is more experientially real.

God did not incarnate Himself in Jesus Christ to remain mysterious, abstract, unapproachable, irrelevant, or distant. He left heaven to engage with you. He determined there was justification for your life so that you could be brought close. He transformed and sanctified you in order to take up residency within you. While it is amazing, this grace is intended to infuse every pore of your soul and each aspect of every day. Jesus Christ incarnated to show you God and make a way for you to live with Him and know Him personally.

Willard says the spiritual disciplines are "simply a matter of following [Jesus] into his own practices, appropriately modified to suit our own condition."

Nineteen times, Jesus said to His followers, "Follow me." When you say you are a follower of Jesus, you don't mean that you can do what He did or that you are a mini version of Him. What you mean is that you emulate the motive and method underlying how He lived, believing that in so doing you will come to know your Father in heaven as your Older Brother, Jesus, came to know Him as a human being.

Jesus also lived by faith, just like you do, in complete dependence upon His heavenly Father. As we examine His practices, you will discover that He practiced a set of disciplines that assisted His heart in accurately reflecting His Father in heaven. As Willard stated, practicing the spiritual disciplines is simply following the practices Jesus followed in order to know God.

Years ago, we lived across the street from a family that was destitute. Their water was cut off, the dad was derelict in his alcoholism, mom worked constantly, and the two boys practically lived at our house. They were constantly bringing me the flat tires on their bicycles to fix—and I was happy to help keep their bikes operational. Then it occurred to me: Why should I fix their flats when I can teach them to fix their flats?

Came the day that Raul pushed his bike up the drive with a flat tire. I told him my new plan and he was enthusiastic. After we removed the tube, I placed Raul between my arms and instructed him to place his hands on mine as I—we together—stretched the tube over the vice on my workbench in order to patch the hole in the innertube.

From extracting the valve stem, to locating the hole, to replacing the tube, the message to Raul was viscerally clear: *Follow Mr. Pres' practices and I will learn.*

Raul learned to fix flats, but in fixing flats he encountered and came to know aspects of me he would otherwise have not known. By placing his hands on mine, feeling my warmth, brushing against the hair on my arms, and feeling my breath on the top of his head, he learned my ways through the practice of repairing the flat tire on his bike.

Jesus said: "Follow me" and I will make you a fisher of men. "Follow me" and I will teach you that in losing your life you find it. "Follow me" and I will show you how to lay up treasures in heaven. "Follow me" and I will demonstrate the power of self-denial. "Follow me" and you will recognize and know the sound of my voice. "Follow me" and I will show you how to die and how to truly live.

On the one hand, it could be said that practicing the spiritual disciplines and personally benefitting from the rigor is a reasonable goal. But that is shortsighted—selfish even. Yes, you are to demonstrate the life of Christ in you, but you are also called to be an ambassador of Christ—His representative in the foreign land of your earthly life.[55]

Dietrich Bonhoeffer, the German pastor who was martyred by Hitler, was asked how it was the German (Lutheran) Church did not resist the Nazis. Bonhoeffer replied it was because the church taught "cheap grace."

Dietrich Bonhoeffer

By cheap grace, Bonhoeffer meant Christian teaching that was lacking in the spiritual disciplines. This perspective was not unique to Bonhoeffer. Grace is free, but cheap grace has

---

[55] Cf.: 2 Corinthians 5:20. Note: An ambassador is a person who resides in a foreign land in order to represent their home country and its interests.

been resisted by the church fathers, the Reformers, and Christian teachers, philosophers, and thinkers through the ages because it misrepresents God's actual, true grace that is magnificent beyond comprehension. Cheapened grace results in a church that is ineffective, shallow, and pithy because cheap grace falls short of costly grace, true grace.

As a member of the Body of Christ living during tumultuous times, it is essential that you not fall from the practice of grace[56] or that you cheapen it by falling short of its daily application and power.[57] In the first place, a cheapening of grace shortchanges your heart's desire. In the second, living a cheapened grace obfuscates—confuses, compromises, obscures—your contribution of Christ in society, that is, your call to be salt and light in the dark world that Jesus spoke about.[58] Thirdly, demonstrating a cheapened grace misrepresents your Older Brother's (Jesus') life, accomplishment, magnificence as King of kings and Lord of lords, and as the supplier of your life, hope, and eternal future.

A vibrant, active, robust church influences society and is both a clarion call for the Gospel as well as societal guardrails to establish and champion a moral people.[59]

---

[56] Cf.: Galatians 5:4.

[57] Cf.: Hebrews 12:14-16.

[58] Matthew 5:13-16.

[59] While a moral society is preferrable to an immoral society, simple morality is not the end goal for Christianity. Rather, a moral society begs the question of why goodness and morality exist, thus fostering an examination of God who is the absolute good and the Gospel which is God's goodness incarnated in Jesus Christ. Without the church's influence, society defaults toward godlessness. As Francis Bacon observed, "They that deny God destroy man's nobility; for certainly, man is akin to the beasts by his body; and if he be not of kin to God by his spirit, he is a base and ignoble creature." Further, a moral society facilitates civil engagement, caring for those less privileged, and embracing those who are struggling. Not only does this engagement guard society against the more egregious of social ills, it too builds a platform from which Christ is presented as the embodiment of grace and truth (Cf.: Jn. 1:17). Jesus said it this way: "By this all men will know that you are my disciples, if you have love for one another" (Jn. 13:34-35). Actively loving others is doing for them the most redemptive thing possible. Sometimes love is a

Bonhoeffer believed that the church must be the conscience of the state and its people. A church—both individual and corporate—imbibing cheap grace fails to influence society, morality, ethics, and the advance of the Gospel.

Bonhoeffer understood that as the spiritual disciplines go, so goes the vibrancy of the Believer, the church collective, and the church's ability to influence society. He elaborated: "Cheap grace is the preaching of forgiveness without requiring repentance, baptism without church discipline, communion without confession, absolution without personal confession. Cheap grace is grace without discipleship, grace without the cross, grace without Jesus Christ."[60]

In his biography of Bonhoeffer, Metaxas writes, "[Bonhoeffer] was trying to get the church to take itself seriously, to grasp what power God had given it, an awesome and frightening power that needed to be understood and used as God intended."[61]

As to that power and the utilizing of it, obedience is the imperative response to grace. From Bonhoeffer's teaching Metaxas observes, "Anything short of obedience to God smacked of 'cheap grace.' Actions must follow what one believed, else one could not claim to believe it."[62] In other words, Christianity has as much to do with how you live as it does with your statement of belief.

The German Church had the appearance of spiritual life. But their religious belief did not translate into practiced, relevant, spirituality in daily life such that German society was influenced. They had faith without works. Thus, their

---

hug. Sometimes love is confrontation. Sometimes love is spoken and sometimes it is the life of Christ in action.

[60] Dietrich Bonhoeffer. *The Cost of Discipleship*. Macmillan Publishing Co. New York, NY. 1980.

[61] Metaxas, Eric. *Bonhoeffer: Pastor, Martyr, Prophet, Spy*. Thomas Nelson. Nashville, TN. 2010.

[62] Ibid.

faith was inert—irrelevant—in that their faith failed to speak into a German society engrossed in the darkness of Nazism.

Reflecting on the cauldron of Nazism, the Holocaust, and political resistance, Bonhoeffer's friend and biographer, Eberhard Bethge, said of Bonhoeffer's influence during those awful days,

> We now realized that mere confession, no matter how courageous, inescapably meant complicity with the murderers, even though... we would preach 'Christ alone' Sunday after Sunday. During the whole time the Nazi state never considered it necessary to prohibit such preaching. Why should it?

> Thus, we were approaching the borderline between confession and resistance; and if we did not cross this border, our confession was going to be no better than cooperation with the criminals. And so it became clear where the problem lay for the Confessing Church[63]: we were resisting by way of confession, but

---

[63] As Hitler rose to power in the early 1930s, the German Protestant tradition of close association between church and state, as well as dislike for the Weimar Republic following World War I, prompted the church early on to support Hitler. However, opposition to Hitler began to grow among some churches and in 1934, led by Martin Niemöller, et al, a synod convened resulting in the issuance of the Barmen Declaration. The defensive posture of those churches opposed to Hitler's control transformed into organized resistance. Later in 1934, meeting in Dahlem, the churches resisting Hitler and the Nazis were named the Confessing Church, thus dividing the German Church into two branches. The Nazis were not threatened by the theologically liberal German Evangelical Church. It was recognized by the government and its Imperial Bishop, the *Reichsbischof*, and had the Nazi's full support. On the other hand, the Confessing Church was perceived a supreme threat and was not only not recognized by the government, the Nazis sought to eradicate it from German society.

To train pastors, Bonhoeffer formed the secret and illegal seminary of the Confessing Church at Finkenwalde in 1935. As Hitler's reign progressed in both power and desperation, the Confessing Church became an enemy of the state and the Nazis sought to destroy it. Martin Niemöller was arrested in 1937. In August 1937, Himmler decreed the education and examination of Confessing Church ministry candidates illegal. In September 1937, the Gestapo closed the seminary at Finkenwalde and by November

we were not confessing by way of resistance.[64]

Encapsulating Bonhoeffer's teaching and the observations of Bethge, Metaxas summarizes: Waiting and looking on is not Christian behavior. It is not living as a Christian.[65]

---

arrested 27 pastors and former students. It was around this time that Bonhoeffer published his best-known book, *The Cost of Discipleship*, a study on the Sermon on the Mount, in which he not only attacked "cheap grace" as a cover for ethical laxity but also preached "costly grace". Bonhoeffer spent the next two years secretly travelling from one eastern German village to another to conduct "seminary on the run" supervision of his students, most of whom were working illegally in small parishes.

Dietrich Bonhoeffer was arrested in 1943. While imprisoned at Flossenbürg concentration camp, Hitler ordered the execution of Bonhoeffer for his association with the Abwehr resistance. Bonhoeffer was stripped of his clothes and led naked to his execution by hanging on April 9, 1944. Bonhoeffer's brother, Klaus, and his brother-in-law, Rüdiger Schleicher, were executed in Berlin on the night of 22-23 April as Soviet troops were already fighting in the capital. Bonhoeffer's brother-in-law, Hans von Dohnányi, was executed in Sachsenhausen concentration camp, on approximately April 9th as well. He was hung using piano wire, just as was Dietrich.

Eberhard Bethge wrote that the SS doctor who witnessed Bonhoeffer's death later recalled a man "devout . . . brave and composed. His death ensued after a few seconds . . . I have hardly ever seen a man die so entirely submissive to the will of God." Bonhoeffer sent one final message, to George Bell in England: "This is the end, for me the beginning of life."

The Confessing Church was decimated by persecution and the conscription of its clergy and laity into military service. In 1948 it ceased to exist when the territorial churches formed the reorganized Evangelical Church in Germany.

Cf.: Editors. "Confessing Church: German Protestant Movement." *Brittanica.com*. Accessed, 12 January 2022.
https://www.britannica.com/topic/Confessing-Church

Cf.: Editors. "Dietrich Bonhoeffer–Finkenwalde Seminary." *Liquisearch.com*. Accessed, 12 January 2022.
 https://www.liquisearch.com/dietrich_bonhoeffer/finkenwalde_seminary

Cf.: Editors. "Dietrich Bonhoeffer." *Wikipedia.org*. Accessed, 12 January 2022.
https://en.wikipedia.org/wiki/Dietrich_Bonhoeffer

Cf.: Editors. "Dietrich Bonhoeffer: Resistance and Execution." *TheBonhoefferCenter.org*. Accessed, 12 January 2022.
https://thebonhoeffercenter.org/index.php/who-is-bonhoeffer/resistance-and-execution

[64] Metaxas. Ibid.

[65] Metaxas, Eric. "Bonhoeffer: Session Two." *The Hub*. Accessed, 12 January 2022. https://www.youtube.com/watch?v=QHNRLmLKCEg

It would be inaccurate to imply that all Christians in Germany lacked spiritual rigor. Bonhoeffer, Niemoller, and countless others resisted the Nazi regime for reasons of faith. It cost many their lives, including Dietrich Bonhoeffer whom Hitler personally ordered executed by hanging on April 9, 1945, just three weeks before he—Hitler—took his own life.

It would also be inaccurate to imply that the parallel between the German Church of the 1930s and the American Church[66] today is a direct correlation. However, it would also be inaccurate to believe there is not a parallel close enough to help diagnose America's turn from God, the church's complicity in society's slide into darkness, and the moral and spiritual imperative that the church must actively engage with its faith and the ever-darkening society in which we live.

America has not embraced a tyrant like Hitler and the church turned a blind eye, but Western society is moving quickly from its moral founding to incorporate degraded, dark, debauched sins of societies that are distant from God. The church is losing—perhaps it has lost—its influence and relevance throughout the Western world.

While we cloister ourselves inside our brick and mortar, our spiritual vibrancy and societal relevance is faded. To those outside the church, we are a voting bloc. The church is designed, called, and equipped to be evangelical, literally

---

[66] My concern with the church in America is not limited to America. Sadly, churches throughout the Western world are afflicted with the same inertia and irrelevance. The question is whether or not the church will "discipline itself for the purpose of godliness" (1 Tm. 4:7). Not long after the collapse of Communism in Albania, I was visiting with the Mayor of Tirana who was a Believer and a man who had suffered greatly for his faith in Christ. At the time, Albania was the poorest country per capita in Europe. He asked, "Preston, how should we in Albania pray for American Christians?" I said, "Please pray that we are freed from the apathy that afflicts our walk with Christ."

meaning: those who carry the Good News[67] of the Gospel. But in civil society, "evangelical" is now pejorative, often linked to notions like uneducated, close-minded, behind, restrictive, regressive, repressive, formative of racism, protectors of its continuance, founded upon and perpetuated by white extremism.[68] As my friend Tony Evans says, "The church no longer has the home field advantage."

Society resents Christians and the church, and for good reason. We declare that we possess a solution for what ails the human soul while keeping that solution to ourselves. We have become dispossessed of the humanitarian and spiritual wherewithal to engage a desperate, writhing, darkening culture.

The innate disposition of all humankind knows intuitively that the grace of God exists—what Pascal called the God-shaped vacuum—and understands that the church is entrusted with the stewardship of this grace. Society further understands, even at a rudimentary level, that the job of the church is to dispense God's grace liberally throughout society. Therefore, it only makes sense that as society becomes less grace-filled, angry and resentful eyes should

---

[67] Cf.: Acts 8:12; 13:32; Romans 10:15-16, et al.

[68] In 2021, Robert P. Jones won an American Book Award for his book, *White Too Long: The Legacy of White Supremacy in American Christianity.* His research is questionable. His techniques less than objective. His questioning is leading in order to substantiate a predetermined thesis. To date there are no parallel studies bringing into question the validity of his thesis that evangelicalism is the foundation of white supremacy. But this suspect research hasn't mattered to the mainstream anxious to place blame for America's schisms. Many major news and journalism outlets embraced Dr. Jones' assertions, not only as true, but as evidence that America's racial and extremist divides have their origins in evangelical Christianity and Catholicism. But not only their origin, their continuation and propagation as well. While evangelicalism is being disparaged and defamed, notable church leaders speak out, not on behalf of the Gospel, but to endorse political positions and candidates. In so doing, these leaders tacitly imply that the church's power is not spiritual but political. The church-at-large remains silent and Christian and Catholic scholars have done nothing to expose and repudiate Dr. Jones' research. To read about Dr. Jones: https://www.prri.org/staff/robert-p-jones-ph-d/

be turned to those entrusted with the dissemination of this great grace who are failing in their stewardship of grace at each turn.

When the church fails to influence society, it is due to the fact that the church has cheapened God's grace by not disciplining itself to distribute a magnificent grace effectively. An undisciplined church cannot, will not, dive into the dark waters of society to carry the life ring of the Gospel to a drowning world.

Thus, the rationale underlying this book.

I determined to write to you about the spiritual disciplines in these pages, not so you can draw closer to God—you are in Him and He is in you—but rather so you can engage the confidence of a robust faith that does not cheapen grace with spiritual talk and an incongruent lifestyle. Just as it is in your heart to believe God for salvation through Christ, it is in your heart to demonstrate your faith with disciplined, rigorous, spiritual performance. But how?

A true faith, a transforming faith, disciplines itself for the purpose of godliness,[69] advocacy for the Gospel, and demonstrations of Christ's life through compelling behavior. The world longs for this from you and resents you when you fail to push back their darkness with the light and life of Christ in you. Who doesn't want a light when they are in a dark place?

Practice of the spiritual disciplines results in two things: First, practicing the fundamentals of the faith positions you on the path that God walks. It is in the engagement of the disciplines that God meets with you, you come to know Him,

---

[69] Cf.: 1 Timothy 4:7.

and that you are able to experientially reconcile who you are with what you do as a child of God and member of His family, the church.

Second, you embrace the disciplines of the faith because it is your heart's desire to accurately and compellingly demonstrate the grace of God, not only for yourself, but for others. When you put your faith into action, society is made thirsty for God, thus positioning you to advocate on behalf of the Kingdom and your Older Brother who is the only water that permanently satisfies thirsty souls.[70]

Your heart longs to know God intimately and closely. The spiritual disciplines are the means by which your heart's desire will find fulfillment.

You are called to live in such a manner that your demonstration of Christ creates thirst for Jesus, light in a dark place, love where there is rancor and hatred, and life where there is death. Practicing the disciplines solidifies your calling while facilitating your application of love, the life of Jesus Christ in and through you.

Faith, and calling, and the realization of your heart's desire necessitate action. Discipline is hard, even unpleasant. Practice is drudgery. Engaging a hostile society is a dicey proposition. But quoting Bethge again regarding the German church's failure to act, "The sin of respectable people reveals itself in flight from responsibility."[71]

The question is clear: How will you live?

---

[70] Cf.: John 4:7-15.

[71] Bonhoeffer. *Life Together*, from the "Introduction" by John W. Doberstein.

Questions and Considerations

1. Early in this chapter, there is this statement: "If you are in Christ there is nothing you can do to cause God to accept you more than He already does. The converse is true as well: There is nothing you can do to cause God to accept you less than He does if you are in Christ." What do you think? Agree or disagree? What if you "discipline yourself for the purpose of godliness" as 1 Timothy 4:7-8 exhorts? Does this affect your standing with God? Your relationship with Him? What if you fail? What if you run your spiritual life—even your earthly life—into the ditch? In an event like this, what happens to your standing and relationship with God?

2. The chapter asks, "What does it mean to have faith?" What's your answer? And whatever your answer is, how does this superintend your daily life moving forward?

3. This chapter draws a tight parallel between the German church of the 1930s and 1940s and today's church in the Western world. Is the parallel accurate, worthwhile? Why or why not? If accurate, then the assertion of this chapter and those cited as references is that a return to the spiritual practices, the fundamental disciplines of the faith, is imperative. Agree or disagree? Why? To what degree or extent? How does your answer guide your life?

FOUR

Introduction to the Spiritual Disciplines

"

"Knowledge without practice is useless. Practice without knowledge is dangerous."

Confucius

There are few good numbers for the church. What positive reports surface are usually focused on a particular church, not the church overall.[72]

Researchers report a mass exodus from church by those Barna terms the committed Believers, meaning: those people who want their faith to be relevant seven days a week. It's sad, but not surprising, that when asked why they

---

[72] Regarding those churches posting positive numbers, a man who studies church life told me, "There's little true growth. For the most part, what is called church growth is actually churches trading members." Of course, there are exceptions. Please do not read me writing categorically or absolutely; I'm conveying a general state of the Western church.

are leaving, these folks indicate it's because the church and its message are no longer relevant.

No longer relevant. To life. To daily struggle. To influencing culture. To knowing God more personally and fully. To work, and faith, and family, and finance, and yes, irrelevant to having fun.

This trend did not start yesterday, or last month, or last year. The decline due to perceived irrelevance has been transpiring for over two decades. Some argue the decline began in the 1960s.

Gallup notes that 69% of Americans were members of a church at the turn of the century. Eighteen years later, in 2018, the percentage had dropped to 52%. Gallup also reports that the number of Americans reporting no religious affiliation has more than doubled since 2000 from 8% to 19%. Church attendance declined by about 10% over the same period across all adult age groups.[73]

But perhaps most alarming is the difference in church attendance between seniors and Millennials. That number is 26%.[74]

Church as it once was is dying.

True, the *living* church, the Body of Christ, is alive in all sorts of places. But the entity through which the Body of Christ can leverage collective influence, benefit from scale, and

---

[73] Jones, Jeffrey M. "U.S. Church Membership Down Sharply in Past Two Decades." *Gallup.com*. April 18, 2019. https://news.gallup.com/poll/248837/church-membership-down-sharply-past-two-decades.aspx.
[74] Ibid.

speak with a powerful voice is in an increasingly steep death spiral.

Reaction to these poor numbers by church leaders has been varied. Most churches of numerical size offer a smorgasbord of programs and a variety of worship service styles. Dress codes have eased, coffee is served, music is louder and more contemporary, common areas have been created, more women in leadership, better lighting in the auditorium, streaming is offered, a smoke machine for ambiance, screens and more screens, topical sermons related to appealing issues, exegetical sermons related to concerns of the day, more enthusiastic greeters, security, refined check-in procedures in the children's wing, remote locations, and so much more.

But the numbers continue to slide. Folks that should be core church members continue to depart. And when asked, the criticism is the same: The church and its message are irrelevant.

But wait.

How can this castigation of irrelevancy be true when the church has modified its programs so aggressively to appeal to a morphing society?

Furthermore, unless we are talking about a church that preaches a social-gospel pablum, it's not possible for the church's message to be irrelevant. How can the Gospel be irrelevant? How can Scripture be meaningless? How can faith fail to guide life and godliness?

If there's nothing wrong with the message, then it must be the delivery. However, see a few paragraphs above regarding delivery and programs. Churches are trying everything to entice people to their campuses.

So, if it's not the message, or the program, and the experiments in delivery aren't making a difference, then the criticism of irrelevance signals that the congregants either don't understand the message, can't manage the message, can't apply the message, or perhaps all of the above.

If you can't implement, or deem something useful—even faith—then only the sentimentalist will bother with the participatory burden of maintaining their overhead cost in time, allegiance, and commitment. In business terms, what Barna, et al, have polled and reported is that committed Believers consider the church and its message a sunk cost. Thus, when asked about religious affiliation, these folks answer, "None." Recall a few paragraphs earlier: This is the group that Gallup reports more-than doubling since 2000.

A business writes off a sunk cost and abandons a failed initiative in order to return to profitability. Said another way, a business abandons a sunk cost in order to preserve and strengthen its fundamental, core business.[75]

If it wishes to survive as a collective institution, it is time for the church to do what businesses do in order to protect their profitability. But first, the church must define and reassert its fundamental reason for existence. If the overhead of all that is the organized church is deemed irrelevant by its customers—both the Believing and

---

[75] To be certain of what I mean by the term, "fundamental," please reference the definition of terms at the beginning of this book. My use of this term is connected to the twelve, spiritual disciplines as basic, rudimentary, and essential. Their practice explored in *Rigorous Grace* has zero to do with the politicized and pejorative title, "Fundamentalist."

unbelieving—then the church must do the hard labor of defining and embracing why it is in existence.

A sunk cost that is excellently conceived, produced, and delivered is still a sunk cost. This is true for business and this is true for the church.

A church program that is excellently conceived and executed but that fails to equip its customer—its congregant—with the transformative power of Jesus Christ, the vibrancy of a personal relationship with God, and the relevance of this to daily life is advancing a spiritually sunk cost.

Just as a business must remain focused on its fundamental business, so the church must maintain fidelity to its fundamental reason for being.

And what is the fundamental business of the church?

As individual Christians, and individuals assembled together with the collective of Believers known as the church, *it is our determined purpose to know Jesus Christ*.[76]

To be clear: Our calling, and the purpose of the church, is *not* to know *about* Jesus, or to know more *about* the Bible, but to truly *know* Jesus and understand the power of His resurrected life in us which transforms us and transforms life in general. If we as a collective, and if we as individuals, were pursuing this fundamental in all aspects of our lives, then our corporate and individual lives would demonstrate

---

[76] Cf.: Philippians 3:7-10. Also, John 17:3, Philippians 1:21, and Jeremiah 9:23-24.

the spiritual vibrancy our hearts desire and culture longs to encounter.

Thus, the church corporate and individual must return to the spiritual fundamentals because these fundamentals are the key to realizing our heart's desire: to know and understand Jesus Christ. Only in so doing will the church return to relevance and influence.

Not to be derogatory, but now is not the time for a study on the four horsemen of the Apocalypse, as interesting as that might be. Now is not the time to explore the spiritual gifts, the nuances of Leviticus, or the intertestamental period. Yes, all Scripture is inspired and profitable, but there are scriptural fundamentals that we must return to and prioritize. After all, if the foundation is weak, the house will not survive.

Fundamental problems necessitate fundamental solutions. That the church has lost its effectiveness is not a negative reflection of the Gospel. It is reflective of a group of people known as the Body of Christ who are consistently failing in their fundamentals. As a result, our reason for being, our heart's desire, our purpose in life is dull, our basic belief obscured, and our faith is deemed irrelevant.

Paul's letter to the Philippians contains a graphic declaration of his determination to know Jesus Christ. The entirety of the passage is contained in chapter three, and I recommend it to you, but for our purposes, here are verses 7-11:

> [7] But whatever things were gain to me, those things I have counted as loss for the sake of Christ. [8] More than that, I count all things to be loss in view of the surpassing value of knowing Christ Jesus my Lord, for whom I have

> suffered the loss of all things, and count them but rubbish so that I may gain Christ, [9] and may be found in Him, not having a righteousness of my own derived from *the* Law, but that which is through faith in Christ, the righteousness which *comes* from God on the basis of faith, [10] that I may know Him and the power of His resurrection and the fellowship of His sufferings, being conformed to His death; [11] in order that I may attain to the resurrection from the dead.[77]

Paul was not only a dedicated man, he was a distinguished religious scholar and a brilliant intellect. His life was a testimony of accomplishment, accolades, and zeal. But note the phrase in verse eight: "...count them but rubbish so that I may gain Christ...." I said above, this passage is a graphic declaration by Paul of his dedication to know nothing but Christ. What he literally writes in this phrase is that by comparison to his determination to know Jesus, all his accomplishments are like refuse. The Greek word translated here as "refuse" is *skubala*, meaning: dung, rotten, crap, the vilest form of human excrement. For Paul, compared to personally knowing and understanding Jesus, everything else he considered to be like a pile of s**t.[78]

Now, you can be offended that I have attributed to Scripture a swear word of disgusting measure. Never mind it's what the author wrote while under the inspiration of the Holy Spirit.

Or, you can stop and consider all that you have, all that you have achieved, all that you are, and all that you hope to be and juxtapose this against your heart's desire to know Jesus above all else. Anything you cling to, anything that distracts

---

[77] Philippians 3:7-11.

[78] Wallace, Daniel B. "A Brief Word Study on Skubalon." *Bible.org*. October 1, 2007. https://bible.org/article/brief-word-study-skuvbalon.

you, any priority, or anything you propose to bring before God to argue your efficacy before Him is an enemy to your soul and *skubala* compared to personally knowing Jesus Christ.

Such is the argument Paul is making in Philippians chapter three. The balance of the chapter is Paul's argument for adopting his outlook, caution regarding those who do not, and his identification of the grave consequences for prioritizing anything in life above, or in addition to, the foundational, singular, priority, and purpose of the faith: knowing Jesus Christ.

Thus, my advocacy for streamlining the magnitude of all that is Christianity in devotion to the purpose and practices that are spiritually fundamental to ensuring that our faith is relevant. That Christianity and the church are deemed irrelevant is not a negative criticism of the faith and the Gospel. It is an indictment that we have lost sight of our purpose as a people. It is a diagnostic revelation of a fundamental failing in the practice of our faith.

While there are Christian resources about the spiritual disciplines, much of the teaching and practice of the spiritual disciplines is infected with legalistic rationale: you *must* read your Bible, pray, contribute, etc. *in order for* God to love you, forgive you, accept you, like you, blah, blah, blah. Legalistic theology sounds reasonable, and is inspirational to some folks, but it is 100% bad theology. What you do obligates God to not an iota of anything.

Like Martin Luther discovered, anything you do to contribute to the completed work of Jesus Christ falls short of the biblical standard of Christ alone (*sola Christos*), through faith alone (*sola fide*). Any hint of anything that you cling to believing it contributes to your standing with God is unchristian. Christ plus anything is not grace. It is an affront to the Gospel and runs fully counter to the biblical standard of Christ and Christ alone.

The key to restoring Christianity's relevance is to return to the practice of our fundamental, spiritual disciplines. It is these practices that place us in position to fulfill our purpose of knowing Christ.

I once asked a friend who played professional football how he diagnosed getting beaten on a play, not as a team, per se, but as an individual player. He said that invariably, when watching the films afterward, he realized he had failed in a fundamental: led with the wrong foot, not had his shoulders square, his head was down, out of position, etc. Being beaten on a play had little to do with his athletic ability and everything to do with failing to practice a fundamental of the game that he first learned playing Junior High ball.

If you think about it, my friend's insight applies to every practice in life, including our spiritual lives.

When there is a mysterious failure to produce or perform, the best wisdom is to return to your fundamentals. For Believers, the fundamentals are what we know as the spiritual disciplines.

But let's be clear: Resolving to do a study of the spiritual practices is not good enough to restore faith to relevance. When you reach the final page of this book, if you have failed to realize that implementation is paramount, then you have missed the point of these pages.

There are two major reasons underlying the criticism of irrelevance: 1) The Gospel, faith, biblical instruction, spiritual training—while each is true, each is also an abstract truth. An abstraction must become concrete before it is useful and can be mastered. A vision needs a strategy. A plan needs management. A goal requires objectives. Action requires measurement and evaluation—and similarly, faith is useless without action.[79]

I'll write more about this as we go, but action steps—the transition from an abstract idea to concrete application—must be instructed, then practiced, and evaluated, not left to the recipient to figure out for themselves. Coaching. Practicing. Disciplining. Evaluating. This is my attempt in these pages.

The strongest pushback I'm receiving to the subject of this book is coming from those most dedicated to teaching the grace of God and our new identity in Christ.

I think they believe that instruction advocating Christian performance is legalistic. I gather they consider evaluation and assessment pure advocacy for performance-based acceptance with God. But I disagree. Strongly! I respect their fear and caution, but a faith that is not applied is irrelevant to daily living.

It is a wonderful thing to be a new creation in Christ who is endowed with a new identity and a pure heart. But no matter how magnificent the truths of the faith are, unless they are implemented into your life, your faith is worthless. Christian performance is mandated by Scripture, not to gain favor with God—only Christ can achieve that for you—but to demonstrate that your faith is real, that Christ is alive, and that God is active and relevant.

---

[79] Cf.: James 2:20.

This is tremendous theology. It has the added benefit of being true! But it is so grand, so magnificent, so mind-boggling, and so incredible that it is an abstraction requiring practice to grasp and make concrete and observable to you and others.

It is an abstraction for me to tell you that Jesus provides salvation—forgiveness of sins, a new identity, the indwelling Spirit, and eternity with God in heaven. You can believe this abstract idea, even believe that it is true, but until you comprehend and identify your sins, repent of them, and declare Jesus Christ your Lord, you won't concretely comprehend what salvation means to you. Until you define your old self prior to salvation, you can't possibly appreciate the death of your old self and the resurrection of your new self—the new you, identified with Christ, and declared true of you by God when you are saved. Further, until you rigorously personalize your new identity, you won't comprehend how the new you treats your spouse, loves your kids, manages professionally, or even enjoys life.

As long as your belief remains abstract, your belief is irrelevant to life. The harder life presses in upon you, the more your soul longs for a relevant faith. As the world's darkness becomes more pervasive, and your faith remains abstract, the more prone you are to decide your faith is irrelevant, doesn't matter, is ineffective, and any further practice of it is a sunk cost.

The second underlying reason we feel our faith irrelevant is, 2) we have failed to understand, implement, practice, and problem-solve the disciplines of the spiritual life. Every aspect of life requires practice.

It is true you are alive as a human being. It is also true that you are alive as a spiritual being. Any undertaking in life, whether physical, mental, or spiritual, requires diligence. You are exhorted by Paul, "The things you have learned and received and heard and seen in me, ***practice*** these things; and the God of peace shall be with you" (emphasis mine).[80]

The Bible is filled with action words and imperative statements to help you comprehend and make spiritual truths relevant. Action in conjunction with faith is not so you gain acceptance with God or enhance your transformation. Action alongside faith is intended to make the abstraction of your faith concrete: that is, a faith that is relevant to life, thought, and belief. Action in conjunction with faith confirms your acceptance with God and mentally secures the fact of your transformation into a new person in Christ.[81]

While your acceptance with God is complete and your standing with God is secure, your struggle to perform your faith—to apply it, to live it, to practice it, to demonstrate it—is irregular and imperfect. In short, you fail in the implementation of your faith with disconcerting frequency. By definition, "practice" implies repeated effort and shaping of your behavior by successive approximation.[82]

---

[80] Philippians 4:9.

[81] Cf.: Romans 12:2.

[82] Learning by successive approximation is called, shaping. Linder and Hale write, "Shaping is a process because it begins with rewarding (reinforcing) a behavior that is somewhat like the final behavior desired. In steps, behaviors that more closely resemble the targeted behavior are rewarded successively, until only the final desired behavior is reinforced." In the life of a Believer, and for our purposes here, knowing Jesus is the stated goal or outcome of walking with Him. Your heart motivates you to act based upon its/your desire to know Christ. As you practice your faith through the spiritual disciplines, the Holy Spirit guides, nurtures, counsels, grows, enlightens–that is, the Spirit reinforces how your performance resembles (or not) your faith and belief. Since your security and standing with God are not performance-based, you are free to fail without divine recrimination. That is, your personal acceptance is not based upon how well you execute the tenets of your faith. Rather, as you fail, the Spirit comes alongside of you and guides

Failure is not pleasant. It's like getting burned: you don't want to do that again. But, failing motivates you to change, modify, reevaluate, and so forth. In actual fact, failure is essential to learning. By declaring you secure in Christ, your heavenly Father frees you to practice implementation during this life, and in so doing, learn Him and His ways. In short, it is through the angst of life while focused on your heart's desire that you come to *know* Him more completely and live the life of faith more congruently.

Epstein's research in his book, *Range*, reveals that true learning, resilient learning, learning that is flexible across multiple fields, *requires failure* to develop—and not just a little bit. Repeated failure is what creates the grit of a resilient, flexible, learned, skill set. "Struggling to retrieve information primes the brain for subsequent learning, even when the retrieval itself is unsuccessful. The harder it [learning] is, the more you learn. Frustration is not a sign you are not learning, but ease is."[83]

The good news is that failure does not change God's acceptance of you. And, failure causes you to learn more deeply such that your spiritual character is tempered with spiritual grit, the steadfast endurance spoken of in Romans,[84] and the set-mind referenced in Colossians that is focused on things above,[85] and the endurance necessary to strip away all impediment to run the race of life and faith.[86]

---

your experiential spiritual development (Cf.: 2 Cor. 7:8-11). As you practice, you grow in your faith and come to know God more personally. See: Linder, James and Hale, Andrea. "Shaping and Successive Approximation in Psychology." *Study.com*. August 25, 2021. https://study.com/learn/lesson/shaping-psychology-concept-examples.html.

[83] Epstein, David. *Range: Why Generalists Triumph in a Specialized World*. Riverhead Books. New York, NY. 2019.

[84] Cf.: Romans 5:1-4.

[85] Cf.: Colossians 3:1-2.

[86] Cf.: Hebrews 12:1.

Practicing the spiritual disciplines does not change you. You are already changed, transformed, and made new by the finished and complete work of Jesus Christ. Rather, the spiritual disciplines change your awareness in that they develop, transform, and enlighten you about the true nature of you. They place you in optimal position so that the Holy Spirit more effectively and efficiently correlates spiritual reality with your earthly experience and vice versa.

You know you have faith in Christ for salvation. The practice of the spiritual disciplines positions you where this faith and earthly practice meld into understanding, applied knowledge, faith in action—in short, the Gospel appropriated and relevant to life and living. Trusting Christ for forgiveness and salvation serve you well in eternity. Trusting Christ for each day's problems[87] serves you well today. Thus, Christ is your hope. Christ is your life. Christ is relevant to everything pertaining to life and godliness, just as Peter wrote.[88]

It's interesting that when James wrote in AD 49, he understood what Epstein wrote in AD 2019: the beneficial role of stress in deep learning, i.e., learning that is resilient and flexible. From chapter one: "Consider it all joy, my brethren, when you encounter various trials, knowing that the testing of your faith produces endurance. And let endurance have its perfect result, so that you may be perfect and complete, lacking in nothing."[89]

Dallas Willard adds that more important than the disciplines themselves is the attitude[90] with which we

---

[87] Cf.: Colossians 2:6-10.

[88] Cf.: 2 Peter 1:3.

[89] James 1:2-4.

[90] Gaultiere, Bill. "Spiritual Disciplines." *SoulShepherding.org*. Accessed, 6 December 2021. https://www.soulshepherding.org/spiritual-disciplines-list/

approach the practice of the disciplines. There are two aspects of attitude pertinent to our explorations.

At the motivational level, successfully practicing the disciplines is an either-or, attitudinal proposition.

You either practice the disciplines as an attitude of the heart that deeply desires to meet with Christ regarding all things related to life and godliness or you practice the disciplines via self-effort for self-centered gain. The first approach empowers your practice with the onboard resource of the Holy Spirit. With the second approach, you are on your own attempting the impossible with God: to improve your standing with Him via self-sufficient performance.

I suppose there is another option as well: not practicing the spiritual disciplines at all. But I doubt you would have picked up this book if that was your attitude.

But this hints at an additional aspect of attitude that Willard had in mind. Discipline is demanding.[91] But the beauty and benefit of discipline is that it enables you to do what is in your heart to do. However, the attitude with which you approach the practice of discipline is a key component in your embrace of the rigor of discipline.

Just after the author of Hebrews writes about running "...with endurance the race that is set before us," he indicates the attitudinal focus essential to stay motivated within the demand of your endurance: "...fixing our eyes on Jesus, the author and perfecter of faith, who for the joy set before Him endured... and has sat down at the right hand of the throne of God."[92]

---

[91] Cf.: Hebrews 12:11.
[92] Hebrews 12:1-2.

Back in the day, when I planned a mountain bike trip to Colorado, I modified my training rides to include hill-climbs out of the Trinity River bottoms to high ground in order to prepare my lungs, legs, and knees for my upcoming ride in the mountains. I suffered in training so I could exult in the mountains.

Sadly, there are many Believers who are educated about the faith, and informed *about* Christ, but they have missed Jesus Christ Himself. They engage spiritual information to satisfy some personal incentive—to participate with their people, learn something new about an interesting subject, to keep pace, to show up within their circle; or perhaps they participate in an effort to enhance their standing with God, which of course is an impossibility.

Why are you motivated to practice the spiritual disciplines?

I believe if you examine your heart, you will realize that your motive is to know Christ and be guided by Him in your life of faith. And the truth of the matter is, awareness of this motive reveals the true desire of your heart.

The means to satisfying your heart's desire—to know Jesus—is the practice of the spiritual disciplines, the fundamentals of the faith, the path Jesus walked in His relationship with God. Upon these fundamentals rest all there is to knowing and understanding your heavenly Father.

With our attitude focused and our goal clear, here we go!

Questions and Considerations

1. As you think about your spiritual life and the spiritual input/teaching you are receiving, are your spiritual life and religious teaching aligned? In short, are what you hear and read spiritually relevant to your Monday-Saturday life? How so—or not?

2. This chapter asserts that practicing your faith is of paramount importance. But as the chapter progresses, it indicates that for practice to do you any lasting good, there must be practice of such rigor that regular failure occurs. The chapter calls this "successive approximation" as defined by the researchers Linder and Hale. So, what do you think about failure being essential to a spiritual life that is relevant to daily life? If you fail—when you fail—where is God? What did He have to do with your circumstantial spiritual failure? When you fail, where does your shortfall place you in proximity to God? Thus, that you will fail is a given. What is to be determined is how you view your failure, what you do in response to your failure, and whether or not you are on your own in failure or if God remains present and accounted for. Thoughts?

3. Toward the end of the chapter, Hebrews 12:1-2 are referenced about "fixing your eyes on Jesus" in order to

endure. What does this fixed focus look like in your life—or what might it look like? How does your focus—or how might your focus—affect your spiritual endurance? Keep in mind, a high-minded ideal is not nearly as effective as a simple application that is routine.

FIVE

The Spiritual Practice of Reading the Bible

"

"The best cure for Christianity is reading the Bible."

Mark Twain

No other book in the history of publishing has been more vilified or praised than the Bible. No other book comes close to paralleling the Bible's readership.

Best-seller lists don't bother listing the Bible. It's the best-selling book every year—and the distance between it and second place is so great that comparison is pointless.

According to *The Economist*, about 100 million Bibles are sold or given away each year.[93] Best estimates are that by 2007 there were between 5 and 7.5 billion copies of the Bible printed—in 349 languages, with at least one book of

---

[93] Editors. "How Many Bibles Are Sold Each Year?" *Reference.com*. April 20, 2020. https://www.reference.com/world-view/many-copies-bible-sold-year-3a42fbe0f6956bb2

the Bible (the Gospel of Mark) being translated into another 2,123 languages.[94] By comparison, the second-best-selling book of all time is J.R.R. Tolkien's, *The Hobbit*. As of 2018, sales were 140.6 million.[95]

And you say, but the Bible is a series of books and *The Hobbit* is just one book. Fair enough. The second-best-selling book series of all time is J.K. Rowling's *Harry Potter*.[96] The series—and its spin-offs—total about 500 million sales. That's enough in royalty payments to make Ms. Rowling richer than the Queen.[97]

Millions versus billions.[98] Both are large numbers to comprehend. Here's some perspective: A million seconds is twelve days. A billion seconds is thirty-one years.

I recommend reading Tolkien and Rowling.

I highly recommend reading the Bible.

The first, most fundamental practice of the Christian life is Bible reading. The Bible's publication numbers are impressive, not because of a marketing campaign, but because the Bible is the inspired Word of God. People read

[94] Editors. "Best-selling Book." *GuinessWorldRecords.com*. Accessed, 7 December 2021. https://www.guinnessworldrecords.com/world-records/best-selling-book-of-non-fiction/

[95] Editors. "List of Best-selling Books." *Wikipedia.org*. Accessed, 7 December 2021. https://en.wikipedia.org/wiki/List_of_best-selling_books

[96] Ibid.

[97] Bonner, Mehera. "What Is J.K. Rowling's Net Worth, You Ask? Welp It Rhymes With More Than a Shmbillion: She's Legit Richer Than the Queen." *Cosmopolitan.com*. January 7, 2021. https://www.cosmopolitan.com/entertainment/celebs/a35110628/jk-rowling-net-worth/

[98] Editors. "Million versus Billion." *Diffen.com*. Accessed, 7 December 2021. https://www.diffen.com/difference/Billion_vs_Million

the Bible because it informs them, transforms them, and offers them a window into God's soul.

This is not my opinion. Rather, the internal evidence[99] of the Bible itself, as well as the practiced eye and study of centuries of experts, and the testimony of multiplied millions of our predecessors in the faith, establish not only the Bible's uniqueness, but its divine inspiration, and power to change the lives of those who read it.[100]

Quoting and amplifying from the Book of 2 Timothy,[101] Warren Wiersbe writes, "Scripture is profitable for doctrine (what is right), for reproof (what is not right), for correction (how to get right), and for training in righteousness (how to stay right)."

The Bible is filled with principles and wisdom. But it is fundamentally more than this. The Bible is the expressed will and desire of God. It contains the mind and heart of God. Reading it with dedication inspires your heart and reveals your true desires. Reading the Bible for personal edification is akin to reading a series of letters from God to you—so personal is the Bible to your life, wellbeing, and heart.

In your heart, which as a Believer is inscribed[102] with the desires of God and is the place of His residence, you deeply desire to know God personally. Your heart and the heart of God are joined, bonded, made one. Your heart and the heart of God can no more be separated than one can be divided into two. What you desire and what God desires are not only

---

[99] Clark, Jason. "How Do We Know the Bible Is the Word of God?" *JasonClark.com*. August 9, 2008. https://jasonaclark.com/how-do-we-know-the-bible-is-the-word-of-god/
[100] Harris, Rabbi Glenn. "Why the Bible Is the Word of God." *GospelOutreach.net*. Accessed, 7 December 2021. https://www.gospeloutreach.net/bible.html
[101] Cf.: 2 Timothy 3:16.
[102] Cf.: Hebrews 8:10.

compatible, they are integrally linked into common motive, intent, and action.

God is so dedicated to this proposition and arrangement that He inspired a book to convey to you in concrete terms what He is like and what is true of you as His child.

While biblical insights, principles, and information about God may interest you, what truly motivates your heart as a Christian is to know God personally,[103] intimately, such that you have confidence that because you are in Him and He is in you, His Word guides, informs, and infuses every aspect of your daily life.

This is your heart's desire.

Let me make certain we are all on the same page: The Bible is a collection of sixty-six books, grouped into an old section and a new section: respectively, the Old Testament and the New Testament. The books are categorized within these two sections according to themes, e.g., poetry, prophecy, gospels, letters, etc.

Sitting down to read the Bible from page 1 to page 1450, like you would read a novel, won't work. That's not how the Bible is organized.

Rather, you will find the Bible more approachable if you read from the New Testament first. It will inform you of the backstory underlying the Old Testament.

The theme of the Bible is God's pursuit of you and all humanity. Throughout the pages, embedded in all types of literature, the Bible demonstrates divine pursuit. The

---

[103] Cf.: Philippians 3:8-10.

centerpiece of all Scripture is the coming of Jesus Christ, the Incarnation, celebrated at Christmas.

If you think about it, whether Christian or not, the world recognizes Jesus as the central person of history. Our calendars are marked as either BC, before Christ, or AD, the Latin abbreviation for *anno domini*, which means in the year of our Lord (Jesus Christ).[104]

This makes Jesus the central figure of the Bible and all of human history.

Given this, it makes sense to begin reading the Bible to understand the life, person, and life-purpose of Jesus Christ. The first four books of the New Testament detail the life of Christ from four, different, literary perspectives. I recommend you start reading with the Gospel of John. You can locate its beginning in the Table of Contents of your Bible.

Whether reading John for the first time, or the umpteenth time, or reading the Bible as a beginner or a long-time student, let me switch gears from *what* to read and offer thoughts about *how* to read, i.e., the spiritual discipline of reading the Bible.

As you would expect, there are numerous approaches to reading the Bible. I encourage you to do some research and experimentation, but a good place to begin is with a daily

---

[104] Development of the calendar is an interesting aspect of historical study. It wasn't until about the sixth century that the church felt the need to refine the calendar, primarily to determine the date of Easter. Even though BC and AD are demarcated by the birth of Christ, the actual year of His birth is not AD 1, but thought to be around 4 BC. There is initiative to replace BC and AD with BCE and CE, meaning: before the common era and common era, respectively. Advocates of the switch argue that BCE and CE avoid religion and are thus not offensive. Even so, what distinguishes either designation is still the birth of Jesus Christ.

reading. I recommend you search for and access YouVersion.com as it offers a selection of reading plans. Find the plan that suits you, and get after it.

It's important to read the Bible in volume. So, read a chapter at a sitting—or more, e.g., the Gospel of John. While the Bible is beneficial in snippets, you will realize greater benefit if you spend a devoted period of time daily to read Scripture and capture the general gist of what it's saying.

When I read Scripture in any volume, large or small, here's what I do: I go to one of my quiet places, open my Bible to where I'm reading, and whisper a prayer along these lines: "Father God, I've come to hear from you by reading your book. Would you please guide my thoughts, help me understand, and please facilitate how I apply what I read? Thank you." Then I begin reading, believing God will answer my prayer.

I also read the Bible in order to study it more deeply. When I do this, I often focus on a paragraph. I will also spend time with a particular verse and its context. Other times, as I study, I consider a single word of Scripture. Such is the profundity of God's Word. Nothing about it is a throwaway. Nothing justifies skimming over or dismissing anything in Scripture.

Although this practice blends somewhat into the next chapter on the spiritual discipline of reflection, I find it helpful—for understanding and retention—to write a one-paragraph summary of what I've read from the Bible. If I've read a longer passage, then my paragraph is truly a summary. If I've read a shorter passage, perhaps only a paragraph from the Bible, then my paragraph is more of a paraphrase. If I've considered a verse or phrase or word, then my paragraph is something of an insightful perspective.

As you study, you have resources that fall into two categories: tools and commentaries.

Tools enable you to do the job of study. Like the tools in your garage, biblical tools sophisticate the kind of study you are able to accomplish. I'll list some of my favorite tools at the end of this chapter.

Commentaries are the studies another person has done and are a combination of their conclusions, opinions, and perspectives. Commentary from a trusted and reliable source—with the operative words being "trusted and reliable"—is valuable... but not up front.

Go to Scripture on your own first. Do your own study. When you first pick up your Bible to read, pray and ask God to speak to you. Let Him speak. Trust that He will do this for you just as you prayed and asked Him to do.

One of the great tenets of Christianity is that the Holy Spirit lives inside you, commissioned to dwell there by God for the express purpose of guiding, teaching, enlightening, and leading you into the truth of Scripture. If you rely first on someone else's commentary when you read Scripture, you essentially bypass the Holy Spirit as your guide and opt for a human commentator.

After you believe you've exhausted your examination of a passage of Scripture, then it makes sense to seek outside input. I've listed a few commentary options at the end of the chapter.

Knowing your Bible is the inspired Word of God, it makes sense to consistently ask yourself a series of questions that will take you deeper into your reading. Here are the four questions I utilize:

1. What is this passage of Scripture saying?
2. What is God telling me about Himself in this passage?
3. What does this passage tell me about me?
4. What do I do with this passage?

What is this passage of Scripture saying? This is a high-level thought, a general idea, a question indicating whether or not you are comprehending. If you realize you are missing pieces of understanding, use your tools (listed below) to see if they provide insight.

For example, in your reading of the Gospel of John, Chapter 18 begins recounting the betrayal of Jesus by one of his followers named, Judas:

> When Jesus had spoken these words, He went forth with His disciples over the ravine of the Kidron, where there was a garden, in which He entered with His disciples. Now Judas also, who was betraying Him, knew the place, for Jesus had often met there with His disciples. Judas then, having received the *Roman* cohort and officers from the chief priests and the Pharisees, came there with lanterns and torches and weapons.[105]

Where is the Kidron? Most Bibles have a collection of maps in the back. Alternatively, open a search engine and inquire, "where is the ravine of the Kidron?" This inquiry typed into

---

[105] John 18:1-3.

your search engine will produce maps and guides to help you envision where Jesus and His disciples were in relation to Jerusalem.

The passage from John says that Judas arrived with the Roman cohort and officers. What's a cohort?[106] A quick search online indicates that Judas showed up with around 500 soldiers. Wow! This unleashes a whole series of questions: Why so many? What were the authorities worried about? How courageous was the Apostle Peter to draw the only sword among the disciples and attack?[107] How did the Romans get involved—and why?

In addition to checking myself for reading comprehension— What is this passage saying?—I always ask: **What is God telling me about Himself in this passage?** After all, since the Bible is God's writing about Himself, asking this question is clearly important.

Returning to John 18: That Judas showed up with 500 soldiers, tells you what about Jesus? That He doesn't resist arrest and chides Peter for drawing his sword,[108] tells you what? When Jesus asks the soldiers who they are looking for, they say, "Jesus of Nazareth." When Jesus says, "I am He," the soldiers all fall backward to the ground.[109] What does this tell you about Jesus?

After considering what a passage tells me about God, I ask: **What does this passage tell me about me?**

---

[106] Editors. "Cohort (military unit)." *Wikipedia.org*. Accessed, 7 December 2021. https://en.wikipedia.org/wiki/Cohort_(military_unit)

[107] Cf.: John 18:10.

[108] Cf.: John 18:11.

[109] Cf.: John 18:4ff.

Continuing to think about John 18: As a Believer, I live in Jesus and Jesus lives in me.[110] Given this, all that Jesus demonstrates about Himself on the night of His betrayal is indicative of the divine resource living within me. How then shall I approach my day and the challenges it brings? The disciples struggled to believe in Jesus such that their belief transformed their behavior. Why? What did they not believe about Jesus and what did they fail to grasp about themselves as Jesus disciples? How do I avoid the same pitfall?

You can sense my final question in the previous paragraph: **What do I do with this passage?** Taking the message of the Bible as true, *how does it guide my life today*?

When my time reading the Bible is over, before I leave my quiet place, I say, "Father God, thank you for your Scripture. I trust you today and I trust you to make the words of your Scripture real and practical to me today. Thank you in advance. Now Father, it's time to rock and roll."

Each day, I consider Scripture. Each day, and with each approach to reading the Bible, I utilize the questions above. This is the discipline—the routine, the practice—of reading the Bible.

Your responsibility is to show up. God's responsibility is to speak to you from His Word. Trust Him and He will tell you about Himself within the pages of His writings.

---

[110] Cf.: John 14:20.

Recommended Resources

Tools:

- Bible versions for you to read: *New American Standard* (most literal translation), *English Standard Version, The Message* (a colloquial translation). I do *not* recommend the *New International Version.*
  - Each of these versions of *The Bible* are available via apps for free, but you will quickly want a hardcopy to read, reference, and mark.
- For daily reading guides and devotional thoughts: YouVersion.com (online or an app)
- For Scripture reference and translation comparisons: BibleGateway.com (online or an app)
- For contextual insights without much commentary, *Unger's Bible Handbook.*
- For word studies: W.E. Vine, *Vine's Complete Expository Dictionary.*
- For reference, lookup, and miscellaneous study resources: BibleGateway.com (set your search to use either the *New American Standard Bible* or the *English Standard Version* of the Bible. Do **not** use the *New International Version* as it is a deeply flawed translation.

Commentaries:

- *Ryrie Study Bible, New American Standard Version*
- *The English Standard Version Study Bible*
  - *The English Standard Version Study Bible* online at ESV.org (see their app also)
- The Blue Letter Bible online: blueletterbible.org

For more on reading and/or studying Scripture:

- Book: Fee, Gordon D. *How to Read the Bible for All It's Worth.* Zondervan. Grand Rapids, MI. 2004.
- Book: Braga, James. *How to Study the Bible.* Multnomah Press. Portland, OR. 1982. This book teaches an outlining method of study and is more in-depth than the book by Dr. Fee.
- Bible Study Fellowship (BSF). Check online for a study group near you, online courses, as well as apps, and Facebook: BSFInternational.org.
- Community Bible Study. Check online for study options: CommunityBibleStudy.org.
- The Hill. Check online for study resources and options: LifeOnTheHill.org.
- Lifetime Ministries. For studies on your true identity in Christ: Lifetime.org.
- Precept Ministries. Check online for study options: Precept.org.
- @Home Bible Study. Check online for study and small group options: AtHomeBibleStudy.com.

Questions and Considerations

1. What is Mark Twain implying with the quote at the front of this chapter: "The best cure for Christianity is reading the Bible?" What does this convey regarding the importance of reading Scripture, understanding what you read, and mastering the application of your reading? Compare and place value upon your personal reading of Scripture and being taught Scripture by others whether spoken or written?

2. How does the manner in which the Bible is organized—thematically versus sequentially—alter how you might approach reading Scripture?

3. This chapter offers four questions to ask of Scripture—all portions of Scripture—in order to assist your comprehension of what you are reading. John 18:1-3 is used as a case-in-point. Select a passage on your own to consider. You might stay within the Book of John, or if another passage comes to mind, go there. Whatever passage you choose (I encourage you to stay within the New Testament for now), pray a simple prayer before you start reading: "Holy Spirit, teach me from your Word, please. Amen." Then, settle down with your Bible, your journal, a legal pad, or at your keyboard. Ask the four questions, and as thoughts come to you, write them down believing that your heavenly Father via the Holy Spirit is speaking to you from His Word.

SIX

The Spiritual Practice of Reflection

> **"**
>
> *"Without proper self-evaluation, failure is inevitable."*
>
> John Wooden

A necessity is a must have, must do: You must read your Bible. You must pray. You must practice reflection, etc.

But, why *must* you practice these spiritual disciplines?

The critic fears that "you must" establishes human behavior as essential to salvation, justification, and sanctification; essential to gaining favor with God; or that improved personal effort can enhance how God feels about you or solidify His acceptance of you. The critic of the spiritual disciplines hears: You must in order for God to (fill in the blank).

Not only are these misunderstandings, but failing to grasp the proper reason, rationale, and motivation underlying the practice of the spiritual disciplines means that you won't practice the spiritual disciplines. That creates a real impediment in living the Christian life. If the disciplines truly are a must, then you must practice them to attain your heart's desire: to know God intimately. Falling short of this grace[111] shortchanges your relationship with God and misrepresents His mercy toward you.

You must implement and practice the spiritual disciplines— not to gain standing or favor with God, but in order to optimally and consistently put yourself in position to practice the faith and implement it practically into your life. In so doing, not only is the abstraction of faith converted into concrete behaviors, but the depth, texture, and vitality of your relationship with God becomes more experientially real, i.e., relevant.

Recall that Richard Foster teaches that the spiritual disciplines are like a path that you walk to meet with God. On either side of the path are precipices. On one side is the drop-off that falls into the abyss of legalism and on the other is the cliff that falls into the abyss of license.

When you became a Christian, your old self died and a new self was raised with Christ.[112] Your dark, wicked heart that Jeremiah wrote about[113] was transplanted with a new heart that is tender toward God.[114] Upon the walls of your new heart are inscribed the desires and laws of God. Jesus Christ lives in you, you live in Him, and the Holy Spirit is called alongside to guide you, comfort you, and intercede for you. In Him, you are sealed, secured, sanctified, and made holy—

---

[111] Cf.: 2 Corinthians 6:1; Galatians 5:4; Hebrews 4:1; and 12:15.
[112] Cf.: 2 Corinthians 5:17.
[113] Cf.: Jeremiah 17:9.
[114] Cf.: Ezekiel 36:26 and Jeremiah 31:31-34. Both of these passages are prophetic, specifically about the new heart a Christian receives at salvation.

absolutely holy enough for God to call you His dwelling place.

Simply stated: this is the Gospel of Jesus Christ.

Any attempt to improve upon the work of Jesus Christ is legalism. Any presumption upon the work of Christ, any disregard, and any manipulation of Christ's work, is license.

Thus, any hint of "you must in order to get God to" is to be renounced as legalism. Any hint of "I will do as I please because I can" is to be renounced as license. Any hint of "I'm spiritually okay, so I will coast" is to be renounced as presumption.

Yet still, "you must" remains integral to the spiritual life. There are over 1500 imperative[115] statements in the New Testament. Rejecting this imperative to act for any reason is a failure to comprehend the deep desire of your heart that is your driving motive as a new creation: to know Jesus Christ.

It is true: Christian performance can be misguided into either legalism or license, with presumption being a form of license. Still, this does not remove the mandate of Christian performance in Scripture.

---

[115] "Imperative" is a grammatical mood in Greek, the original language of the New Testament. An imperative statement conveys an order, strong intent, or a driving desire connected to wellbeing, fulfillment, or benefit. However, the Imperative Mood is classed among the speculative moods in Greek, not because the intent is uncertain or unclear, but because it is unknown whether you—the reader, the hearer—will choose to act on the Imperative or not. Thus, the intent of God is clear in Scripture. Whether or not it is applied is uncertain in that it is dependent on your determination to obey and act. Certainty is dependent on you determining to obey and act.

Paul tells the Ephesians that as God's workmanship they are created for good works.[116] He wrote Titus and said that since Believers are possessed with a pure heart, they are therefore zealous for good deeds.[117] To accommodate a heavenly theology that does not necessitate complementary action on earth is in fact Gnosticism, the ancient heresy separating spirituality and physical behavior in order to permit license and absolve Believers of personal responsibility.[118]

Thus:

You must—but you must because it is in your heart to do so.

You must—because it is your true desire.

You must—because it is part of your nature to be obedient to God.

---

[116] Cf.: Ephesians 2:10.

[117] Cf.: Titus 2:14.

[118] Charles Colson notes, "English historian Paul Johnson contends that the great obstacle to modern belief in human sin began with the loss of belief in individual responsibility. This elimination of individual responsibility has encouraged the corresponding utopian belief in man's collective perfectibility." It is alarming how aggressively America is pursuing the utopian ideas of Socialism and Communism, even at the expense of the rule of law, social justice, and civil discourse, not to mention concerted efforts to overthrow Constitutional law and American government. Colson continues, "Utopianism always spells disaster because 'the utopian holds that, if the goal is goodness and perfection, then the use of force is justified,' as Thomas Molnar writes. With God dead or ill [due to the church's retreat from societal engagement and influence in secular culture], men and women are stripped of their source of dignity and reduced to sophisticated beasts. At the same time, society denies individual sin, blaming all social ills on environment, and illogically assumes human perfectibility." Is this not what we are currently witnessing as America's prisons are emptied, critical race theory is advanced, and individuals are absolved of personal responsibility? Thus, the critical importance of the church in society. Ref. Colson, Charles. *Kingdoms in Conflict.* Co-publication of William Morris and Zondervan Publishing House. Grand Rapids, MI. 1987.

You must—because it is essential to making the abstraction of faith concrete in your life.

You must—because it is the means to knowing God personally versus knowing about God religiously.

You must—because this equips, prepares, and positions you to be salt in an unsavory world, light in a dark place.

You must *not*—when doing so wounds your heart, sabotages true desire, accommodates disobedience, tolerates an abstract faith, justifies disbelief/irrelevance, and compromises the vibrancy of your walk with Christ.

The litmus test for performance is motive: Why am I doing what I do?

If you perform to improve your standing with God, your motive is misguided. How can you improve upon the finished accomplishments of Jesus Christ?[119]

If you perform because you recognize that doing so is the driving force of your new heart, then your motive is pure.

Returning to Foster's image: As a child of God, you place yourself on the path of the spiritual disciplines because you are motivated to know Christ more clearly, with deeper understanding, and greater earthly conviction. You practice the disciplines because you desire for all that is true of God, and you as a new person in Christ, to inform, guide, and permeate all that you do.

---

[119] Cf.: Colossians 2:9-15; Hebrews 10:10.

To be clear: You can't do anything for God. The notion of doing anything for God implies that God is poor enough that He needs your assistance.

The thing God deeply desires from you is your dedication to knowing Him foremost, above all else, in this life. The spiritual disciplines are your ticket to this increasing knowledge, understanding, experiential, and reflective closeness.

The first discipline—or practice—we explored was the spiritual practice of reading the Bible. To make reading Scripture more practical and beneficial, we formulated a series of four questions to ask:

- What is this passage saying (am I comprehending)?
- What is this passage telling me about God (who is God)?
- What is this passage telling me about me (as a Christian, as a new person, as a child of God)?
- What do I do with this passage (how does this guide my life)?

Building on the practiced discipline of reading the Bible, the second discipline is the spiritual practice of reflection. It capitalizes on the four questions asked while reading and studying the Bible.

Comprehension is important. Retention—remembering what you read—is essential. Application is imperative. Failing in these means fundamental aspects of your salvation are pithy, unfounded, and irrelevant to daily life.

Much of Christian input traditionally comes in the form of an oral presentation: a sermon. While inspirational, maybe educational, here's what research demonstrates:

Immediately following a ten-minute presentation, listeners only remember 50% of what they heard. By the next day, their retention drops to 25%. A week later, it's only 10%.[120]

Is it any wonder that the people in the pew struggle to implement what they hear on Sunday? After a while, is it any wonder that the people in the pew decide the message they're hearing isn't relevant?

Comprehension—true understanding, learning, proficiency, and acquisition of knowledge—increases the more of your senses that are engaged.[121]

The beauty of reading the Bible is, a) you are *seeing* the words on the page, and b) *hearing* God speak to you from His writings.

Adding the discipline of personal reflection to your reading means that a third sense is engaged. When you make notes or journal your reflection on the four questions, your writing adds the sense of *touch*.

Said another way, by practicing reflection, you interact with the information you read. Doing so empowers hearing, not to mention the benefit of deeply processing what you read in collaboration with the Holy Spirit's guidance.

If you verbally dictate your thoughts into a document, or verbally review what you've written, you add yet another layer of sensory association with your studies. If you study

---

[120] Malcolm, Jack. "How Much of Your Presentation Will They Remember?" *JackMalcolm.com*. January 15, 2019. http://jackmalcolm.com/2012/08/how-much-of-your-presentation-will-they-remember/

[121] Abel, Judy. "How Sensory Memory and Your 5 Senses Can Improve Study Effectiveness." *PocketPrep.com*. October 3, 2019. https://www.pocketprep.com/posts/how-sensory-memory-and-your-5-senses-can-improve-study-effectiveness/

individually, and then get together with a small group who've also studied the passage, your verbalization and the dialogue with others further enhances your mastery of the passage.

Some study methods, like Precept,[122] encourage you to illustrate what you read with various images, diagrams, and color-coded highlights. This adds another layer of sensory connection in addition to networking the stylistic categories of how you learn: auditory, visual, tactile, and reading.[123]

Let me repeat: The more of your senses you incorporate into your study, the greater your retention and comprehension will be.

Even if you learn in one, primary manner, by cross-referencing your learning style with other learning styles, you will better understand how a concept is assembled and how durable it is to your analysis. Conceptual cohesion, paired with deep learning, creates mastery of a subject that is meaningful, resilient, and flexible.

By *meaningful*, I mean that you derive knowledge, understanding, and wisdom from your learning. By *resilient* I mean that your learning becomes conviction that weathers question, doubt, and criticism. By *flexible*, I mean learning that is readily applicable and associative across multiple platforms, arenas, and aspects of life.

It is one thing to ask yourself the four questions as you read your Bible. It is another to *actively* reflect on a passage by journaling what you see, hear, and consider—and I trust you

---

[122] Cf.: Precept.org.

[123] Cf.: Malvik, Callie. "Four Types of Learning Styles: How to accommodate a diverse group of students." *Rasmussen.edu*. August 17, 2020.
https://www.rasmussen.edu/degrees/education/blog/types-of-learning-styles/

grasp that "journaling" is broadly defined, not specifically the act of writing in a blank book, although I'm a strong advocate for stringing words together on a page. I have friends who supplement their journaled words with drawings of their musings and interactions with God. Other friends essentially scrapbook a journal that elucidates their time spent with God. Others, whose journals are photographs depicting what they've read and heard from time with God. The important thing is to interact with Scripture, with God, and with your heart in a tangible, active, reflective manner. Wordsworth said, "Fill your paper with the breathings of your heart."

There's nothing wrong at all with reading the Bible for pleasure or casual reading. If you require your reading to be intense each time you approach Scripture, it is likely to become a drudgery. The key is to vary your approach to reading but to understand mastery comes from diligent practice to make application.

I'm a fan of words on a piece of paper. Writing requires you to discipline your thoughts.

Take note of your thoughts. Listen to a conversation. Your mind leaps and jumps. Conversation is comprised of incomplete sentences, nuance, assumption, and presumption, and if face-to-face it relies on another's body language and facial expression to let you know whether or not you are communicating.

The written word is not this way.

Sentence fragments. Incomplete sentences. Assumptions. Presumptions. Leaps in logic. None of this works when you write. The written word must be logical, sequential, rational, and thorough or the reader gets lost. This is true even if you are the reader of your own writing—and this is the power of journaling.

By disciplining your reflections into written words, you force your reading and personal reflection to make sense. If it doesn't, you are forced to reconsider and rewrite.

Now I'm a writer, so I write words when I journal. But I write in my journal differently than I do when I'm writing to you. My published words are edited for public consumption. My journal is not.

When I journal, I write like I do when I'm writing a first draft. That is, I write what is in my head and heart to write. I correct spelling, and I review what I've written for continuity, but I don't do what I call wordsmithing. This means I gain the benefit of disciplined writing without enduring the tedious work of editing.

In learning theory, one of the primary resources used to teach people how to reason is the tool of compare and contrast. This is a form of abstract reasoning versus the more direct forms of inductive and deductive[124] reasoning.

---

[124] Inductive: "Inductive reasoning is the act of using specific scenarios and making generalized conclusions from them. Also referred to as 'cause-and-effect reasoning,' inductive reasoning can be thought of as a 'bottom up' approach. For example, you might observe that your older sister is tidy, your friend's older sister is tidy and your mom's older sister is tidy. Inductive reasoning would say that therefore, all older sisters are tidy."

Deductive: "Deductive reasoning is the act of making a generalized statement and backing it up with specific scenarios or information. It can be thought of as a 'top down' approach to drawing conclusions. For example, consider the statement 'all apples are fruits.' When you introduce a specific piece of information like 'all fruits grow on trees', you can then deduce that all apples grow on trees. Another classic example of deductive reasoning is the following formula: If A = B and B = C, then A must equal C."

Keiling, Hanne. "Inductive vs. Deductive Reasoning." *Indeed.com*. October 11, 2021. https://www.indeed.com/career-advice/career-development/inductive-vs-deductive-reasoning

For example: Let's say you are studying Romans 6:4-7 and read:

> ⁴ Therefore we have been buried with Him through baptism into death, so that as Christ was raised from the dead through the glory of the Father, so we too might walk in newness of life. ⁵ For if we have become united with *Him* in the likeness of His death, certainly we shall also be *in the likeness* of His resurrection, ⁶ knowing this, that our old self was crucified with *Him*, in order that our body of sin might be done away with, so that we would no longer be slaves to sin; ⁷ for he who has died is freed from sin.

This passage is an example of both deductive and inductive reasoning: Since Christ died and your old self was crucified with Him, you deduce that your old self died. The inductive aspect of the verse is: Since your old self died in Christ and your body of sin with it, you understand inductively that you are freed from sin.

But what if you compare and contrast as well: What was your old self? What was it like? Why did God hate it so much that Christ had to die? Therefore, in contrast: What is your new self? What is it like? Does this explain why God accepts you as unblemished? Then, by comparison: To live as though your old self is alive creates internal conflict because you are new. By comparison, new people live new lives that, by contrast with the old life, exemplify Christ's life as they walk in the power of the Spirit.

When you get to verse eleven, "Even so, consider yourself dead to sin but alive to God in Christ Jesus," the passage makes sense, i.e., it is relevant. You know that by considering yourself dead to sin, you are focused on how

Scripture is implemented into your life. Based upon this passage of Scripture and the disciplined practice of reflection, when sin presents temptation to you, your application is, "No! I'm dead to you, sin. I'm alive to God in Christ Jesus. Father God, I obediently present myself to you as a righteous person because of Jesus' work in my life."

Note: This declarative statement is the summary outcome of your reflection on Romans 6:4-7... as well as your application from Romans 6:12-19.

Because you have died and are made new, you are freed from having to go along with sin's enticements. You are also free—and responsible—to live obediently, in concert with what is true. Thus, your reflective understanding of what is true of God, what is true of you, along with what you know of sin, guides and coaches your application of spiritual truth inside your daily life.

Inductive, deductive, and comparative reasoning all build layers of comprehension, memory, and applicability. This further increases the resiliency and depth of your learning.

Your Christian life is steady, you are confident, and your disposition is secure because you have learned at a deep level—by practicing these two disciplines. Thus, who God is, who you are, and how this comprehension is applied can now be implemented.

This is faith in action, faith that is relevant.

Questions and Considerations

1. This chapter begins with an exploration of motive: Why are you doing what you are doing? How do you determine motive? How do you establish—or decide upon—motive? These questions suggest that you have control over your motive. Your thoughts on this? Do you or don't you?

2. All of the spiritual disciplines have within them the concept of practice, an initiative that you take with a declared trust in the Spirit to empower you, not to enhance your standing with God, but to put you in place to communicate with your heavenly Father about matters important to you both. But even when trusting the Spirit within, the action step remains yours to take. Footnote 118 elaborates on the importance of personal responsibility, a freedom and response-ability that is more in question—even compromised—today than in recent history, certainly in the West. Clearly, this chapter is declaring personal responsibility a spiritual endowment and privilege, not a political one. Assuming the importance and value of personal responsibility, what do the spiritual practices, and the freedom to personally implement them, require of you? Is there any other way to realize your heart's desire to know and understand God (cf. Jeremiah 9:23-24a) than to assume personal responsibility to reflect upon the relationship

between Him and you? Where does your personal responsibility and the guidance and coaching of the Holy Spirit begin and end?

3. Reflection is an essential spiritual practice; this is the thesis of this chapter. How will your practice of reflection take shape—what will it look like? Will you journal, contemplate, describe what you reflect upon? How will you retain the insights you gain through reflection?

SEVEN

The Spiritual Practice of Confession

> ## "
> *"A confession has to be part of your life."*
> *Ludwig Wittgenstein*

Theologians and philosophers have long debated what composes a human being. While science ponders neurons, DNA, and cellular structure, metaphysics wonders whether humans are comprised of two parts or three.

All agree that humans have a body, and all agree that we are possessed of some combination of a soul and/or spirit. But is the soul distinct from the spirit or are soul and spirit the same and any distinction semantics?

For our purposes related to the spiritual practice of confession, I endorse the tripartite view of us: Humans are a trichotomy composed of body, soul, and spirit.

1 Thessalonians 5:23 references, "...your spirit and soul and body...." Literally translated, this phrase reads, "...the spirit and the soul and the body...."

In the original language of the New Testament, when a sequence occurs—spirit, soul, body—and each element in the sequence has its own definite article ("the"), and each is separated by a conjunction ("and"), then each element listed in the sequence is distinct from the other.

So, according to this passage, humans are comprised of three, distinct parts: spirit, soul, and body.

If you were to draw a diagram of a human, it might look like a three-layer cake. Of course, it's not possible to literally divide a human into three parts, but the distinction helps us understand how we function.

It's easy to define what we mean by body. At this moment, my body is tapping on my keyboard to produce this composition of words that you are reading or listening to.

But then the definitions become more difficult.

By soul, I mean that part of you that thinks (mind), feels (emotion), and makes decisions (will). Psychologists describe the soul as your personality, an aspect of you that makes you uniquely you.

So, at this moment, the only one of me in the history of humanity is thinking, feeling, and deciding about what I want to communicate. On your end, you are thinking (mind) as you read my words. Hopefully, you are inspired (emotion) to decide (will) that you will implement the practice of confession.

For Christians, the spirit is the place where the Holy Spirit dwells and is the aspect of you that relates to God. Upon your salvation, you are endowed with a new spirit and made alive with Christ. Just as Jeremiah and Ezekiel prophesied,[125] when you become a new creation, you are given a new heart, and upon the walls of your heart, God has etched His desires so that you desire what your Father in heaven desires.

Together, the redeemed soul and spirit define what Romans[126] terms the new self, or what Corinthians[127] describes as the new creation. When you die physically and go to heaven, you will retain your spirit and soul while receiving a new body.

So, what does this have to do with the spiritual disciplines?

"Spiritual" identifies all that is true about you and your relational standing with God.

"Disciplines" define how your soul exercises making truth practical, applicable, and demonstrable. Spiritual truth is a belief. Discipline is a belief applied consistently, just as the quote by Jim Collins at the front of this book states.

The spiritual disciplines are rooted in spiritual truth that you practice in order to align your belief and behavior. Not only do you come to know and understand God more fully as you practice the spiritual disciplines, you also build new habits of behavior that are less reflective of your old self and more reflective of your new self.

---

[125] Cf.: Jeremiah 31:31-33 and Ezekiel 36:26.
[126] Cf.: Romans 6:4-6.
[127] Cf.: 2 Corinthians 5:17.

Repetitive discipline—that is, diligent and determined practice—engages the spiritual fundamentals with enough frequency and duration of time to transform your habitual ways of thinking, feeling, and deciding to behave to better reflect what is true. The labor you expend to perfect your discipline is reflective of your heart's desire to know God personally as opposed to merely being informed about Him. While you are transformed and made new as a person, the spiritual disciplines assist you in understanding, problem-solving, and applying this truth and your heart's desire throughout your life and conduct. This is a learned life-skill, and like any other skill, the more you practice, the better your execution becomes. That is, the more time you spend practicing what is true, the less time you spend performing what is not true.[128]

More specifically, what does this examination of your spirit and soul have to do with your spiritual practice of confession?

After Paul establishes in Romans 6 that the old you was crucified with Christ and a new, transformed you was raised with Christ, he launches into the ramifications of this truth. Since you are a new person who is dead to sin, it only makes sense that you consider this spiritual reality true and applicable in your daily living through sincere obedience.[129]

By "obedience," Paul means that you will obey whomever you are obedient to, either of sin resulting in death or the Spirit resulting in righteousness.[130] Paul is asking who you will *confess* allegiance to as a new person, filled with the Spirit, dead to sin, and alive to God. It is true that you are a

---

[128] In thinking about how learning occurs, it might be helpful to review footnote 82 on p.68 in the chapter, "Introduction to the Spiritual Disciplines."

[129] Cf.: Romans 6:1-19.

[130] Cf.: Romans 6:16-18.

new person. What is to be determined, or demonstrated, is whether you will behave like you did when you were dead to God or whether you will behave like the new individual you truly are as God's child.

What will your confession be?

What is true in your spirit is worked out in your soul. What is spiritually true must be *disciplined* in order for you to consistently align belief and performance. You cannot learn the ways of God and consistently implement the indwelling life of Christ if your daily *practice* is haphazard, ill-defined, mysterious, or unresolved.

Paul writes later in Romans[131] that you will be transformed by the renewing of your mind. Since he established your spiritual transformation six chapters earlier, the transformation Paul refers to here can only refer to an experiential, demonstrable transformation. He is pressing you to make certain your soul and spirit are consistently aligned in belief and behavior. As you do so, the verse notes that when your spirit and soul are in concert, you will "prove" through practiced obedience what is true spiritually.

As you can see, it is true that you are transformed—sanctified—when you become a Christian. Spiritually, you are a new person. But it is equally true that this spiritual transformation must be disciplined via practiced obedience in your soul for it to do you any transformative good in terms of your daily experience.

Thus, there is tension between your spirit and your soul. Both aspects comprise your new self, but trusting Christ

---

[131] Cf.: Romans 12:2.

daily is a dynamic process driven by obedience and declaration—the *confession* of that which is true in order to facilitate how you desire to live.

God speaks to your soul via your spirit. If you obey, this is what Scripture calls walking in the Spirit.

But this isn't the whole picture. Satan also speaks to your soul, but he does so via what Scripture calls the law of sin, or the principle of sin, or simply sin. If he successfully deceives you into believing what he tempts you to adopt, you are doing what Scripture calls walking after the flesh.

Truth versus deception. Obedience versus disobedience. Walking in the Spirit or after the flesh.[132]

When you implement the first discipline, reading and studying the Bible, you fill your mind with truth about who God is, who you are, and what Scripture tells you about applied faith.

When you implement the second discipline, personal reflection and journaling, you seize upon multiple ways of learning such that what you read in the Bible is not only personal, but your study forms deep learning that is resilient, flexible, and integrated throughout your life.

The third discipline, confession and self-examination, infuses into your soul the power of personal declaration and genuine humility that is reflective of what is spiritually true.

Foster writes: "Spiritual disciplines are habits, practices, and experiences that are designed to develop, grow, and strengthen certain qualities of spirit—to build the 'muscles'

---

[132] Cf.: Galatians 5:16-17.

of one's character and expand the breadth of one's inner life."

The McKay's write, "...the spiritual disciplines are not a way to earn one's way to heaven, but rather are the means by which to put oneself in position to more fully receive [experientially] that grace."

When you confess in your soul what is true in your spirit, you position yourself to be counseled by God's Holy Spirit as you live-out your daily life. In this way, your confession is akin to a stated allegiance, a vow, a pledge, a statement of belief. Your confession engages your mind's thinking, your emotion's passion, and your will's resolve.

The spiritual discipline of confession serves you well because it synchronizes the new you with how you live while positioning you to be counseled by the Spirit regarding God's ingenuity in the way He transformed you.[133]

But this isn't the only benefit of the practice of confession as a spiritual discipline.

A confession can also be an admission of failure and sin: "Father God, I have sinned against you and my true self by (and you name what you did wrong). I apologize, Father."

It is true that because of the completed work of Jesus Christ, you are a forgiven person.[134] So, while the intent may be

---

[133] The formative process I'm describing is stated in Philippians 2:12: "Work out your salvation in fear and trembling." The passage is not advancing a works-based salvation. Rather, it is addressing the experiential need you have to apply your belief, i.e., to work it out, figure out how it works, and relates to life. So, the exhortation in Philippians 2:5ff to adopt the same attitude Jesus exhibited gets "worked out" by the guidance given in 2:12ff.

[134] Cf.: 1 John 2:12; Ephesians 1:7, 4:32; Colossians 1:14, 2:13. Note in each of these passages the past tense use of forgiveness.

good, going to God with requests for forgiveness is not only a misunderstanding of Christ's work, but candidly it is a slap in the face of God. By asking forgiveness, you confess in your asking a doubt about the efficacy of Christ's accomplished forgiveness of you and your sins.[135]

In this use of the discipline of confession, you are served by your declaration, not of what is true, but of the incongruity between what you did—the sin you committed—and what is true. In this way, confession is not only a statement of personal responsibility for disobedience, but making the

---

[135] Inevitably, the if/then statement in 1 John 1:9 is put forward to cast doubt upon the forgiveness accomplished by Christ and to establish a contingent forgiveness dependent upon your dedication to confession. John writes, "If we confess our sins, He is faithful and righteous, so that He will forgive us our sins and cleanse us from all unrighteousness" (1:9).
So, which is it? Are you totally forgiven or is your forgiveness dependent upon your confession?
In the first chapter of his book, John is writing to address the heresy of Gnosticism. These folks [the Gnostics] believed there was no connection between what they believed was spiritually true and what they did in life. John is setting up a series of hypothetical scenarios to get the attention of Gnostic adherents. The if/then statements by John in 1 Jn. 1:5-10 are ify ifs. They are for instances. Hypothetical notions. They are "let's say for example" statements.
Not to belabor the point, but there are two, major issues with using 1 John 1:9 as an applicable formula for forgiveness.
First, if John intended verse 1:9 to be his instruction on how forgiveness is gained, then he contradicts himself in the next chapter when he writes, "I am writing to you little children, because your sins have been forgiven you on account of His name" (2:12). Note the past tense: "have been forgiven."
Second, if you are not already completely forgiven, then a significant aspect of your standing with God is contingent upon something required of you. Your salvation is not by grace through faith as Ephesians 2:8 states, but is supplemented by your dedicated confession each time you sin. If this is the case, then the biblical books of Ephesians, Romans, Galatians, and Hebrews come unraveled like a cheap rug and the "finished" work of Christ is unfinished and is proven a myth.
If your forgiveness as a Christian is not fully accomplished in Christ, then Christ's life is a sham, the covenants of Scripture are proven invalid, and your eternal future is dependent upon your resourcefulness. Good luck with this theology if you embrace it. You're going to need it.

confession requires humility, thus reminding you that your reliance in all ways must be upon Christ and Him alone.

As Dietrich Bonhoeffer thought about the function and role of the church, and the spiritual discipline of confession in particular, he wrote in *Life Together* that sharing confession of sin with another person not only promotes the help and alliance from a trusted friend, but it also sustains the humility of knowing that without utter reliance upon the indwelling Holy Spirit, we are most vulnerable to deception. Quoting Bonhoeffer: "A man who confesses his sins to a brother knows that he is no longer alone with his dark night of secret sin."[136] And here's this from the Book of James: "Therefore, confess your sins to one another, and pray for one another so that you may be healed."[137]

Thus, confession keeps you honest about this life and the life that is yours in Christ. Additionally, your confession reveals incongruity between your belief and your behavior. Once this is clear, you are now informed regarding what you need to do in order to correct course. "Knowledge is power," just as Francis Bacon observed in *Meditationes Sacrae* (AD 1597).

As we have already hinted, confession can also be a declaration of what is true, of true intent, true desire, and true obedience. In this use, confession is a statement of belief to justify or acclaim why you do what you do.

There is the famous confession of Martin Luther while on trial for his reformative theology: "I cannot and will not recant anything, for to go against conscience is neither right nor safe. Here I stand, I can do no other, so help me God.

---

[136] Bonhoeffer. Ibid.

[137] James 5:16.

Amen." Note that Luther's declaration is not only a statement. It is also a prayer.

It is sobering to consider, but millions of Christians around the world are making such confessions of faith, knowing that in doing so, they destine themselves for torture, imprisonment, and for many, death.

Confession is a powerful, potent tool in that it assists your soul's ability to distinguish your spiritual desire from the allure of the world, and in confessing the distinction, state your heart's true intent, conviction, desire—indeed, your sincere confession. In addition, confession summons the courage and resolve that reside deep within your soul.

Regarding this grit that resolves and drives your soul, David wrote[138] that "deep calls to deep." He is poetically conveying that the mercy of God, what he identifies as God's longsuffering, infuses his prayer, his comfort, his security, and his future. How deep is God's mercy and longsuffering? To connect with God in the depth of His mercy reveals that your soul is capable of such depths.[139]

---

[138] Cf.: Psalm 42:6-8.

[139] As noted earlier, your spirit and soul comprise your new self, the redeemed you. Should you die today, your spirit and soul are heaven-ready. The earthly conflict you sense within your soul indicates that it longs for release from the compromise of this world, to see clearly, and live truly without impediment. Plato believed that the soul was designed to fly with God in the realm where He soars. Although it is unlikely Plato had access to the Hebrew Scriptures describing the fall of mankind in the Garden of Eden, he nevertheless writes of the soul's demise and it being cast down to earth. The soul's longing for wisdom and beauty, Plato believed, is the soul's haunting reminiscence of what it lost in its fall from God and its desire to once again soar with God according to its design. With your redemption in Christ, your soul regained its wings. This world is neither your home nor destiny. Longfellow wrote, "Dust thou art, to dust returnest, / Was not spoken of the soul" (cf. "Psalm of Life"). You are not simply the recipient of grace and mercy. You are now—in your soul—reconstituted by Christ to live vigorously, vibrantly, in constant harmony with Him who is grace and mercy. You long to fly, to touch the face of God, and soar where He soars.

David's poem is a confession. That he wrote down his confession in song is a demonstration that a patriarch of our faith practiced the spiritual discipline of confession. Here's the passage:

> O my God, my soul is in despair within me;
> Therefore I remember You from the land of the Jordan
> And the peaks of Hermon, from Mount Mizar.
>
> Deep calls to deep at the sound of Your waterfalls;
> All Your breakers and Your waves have rolled over me.
>
> The LORD will command His lovingkindness in the daytime;
>
> And His song will be with me in the night,
> A prayer to the God of my life.[140]

Confession declares what is true of God, true of you, and true of your heart's desire. Such declarations affirm, inspire, remind, establish, and summon your transformation into transformed action.

Chapter 3 of Colossians begins, "Therefore if you have been raised up with Christ, keep seeking the things above, where Christ is, seated at the right hand of God. 2 Set your mind on the things above, not on the things that are on earth. 3 For you have died and your life is hidden with Christ in God."[141]

"Things above." Things that are spiritually true, not the deceptiveness of earthly life. Why? Because you died in Christ and your new life is secured with Christ in God's

---

[140] Psalm 42:6-8.
[141] Colossians 3:1-3.

covenant. Given what is true, set your mind—confess, declare; discipline your thoughts; think about what is true.

Thus, to confess what is true, is to declare: I am a new person. I am accepted, loved. I am a person of worth. I am significant. I am secure. I am victorious. I am forgiven. There are several hundred statements in Scripture that define and articulate spiritual truth about you. The whole of Scripture tells you what is true about God.

What then is the discipline of confession in order for these spiritual truths to be made practical?

You state spiritual truths aloud. You write them in your journal. You jot them onto sticky notes and paste them to your mirror, on the frig, on your dashboard, on your computer monitor—all places you frequent so you will be frequently reminded to confess within your soul what your spirit knows is true. Memorize them, and the Scriptures that go along with them. Recite them as you run, walk, or drive. When under duress, declare them in your mind and with your tongue.

It's important for confession to be accurate and specific.[142]

---

[142] In the Appendices you will find a chapter titled, "The Battle for Your Soul." It contains two worksheets: 1) "The Flesh Inventory" and 2) "My True Identity in Christ."
Although you are a Christian and desire to please God, you experientially find that it is deceptively easy to live contrary to your heart's desire and your true self, i.e., you sin against God and live hypocritically to your true person. This is not uncommon. In fact, Paul wrote about his struggle with this in Romans 7:14-25.
This struggle you experience is the conflict between walking after the flesh versus in the power of the spirit (ref. Gal. 5:16-17). The reason temptation is so compelling is that your temptations correlate with your habitual patterns for living independent from God, i.e., what the Bible terms, your flesh: habitual patterns for thinking, feeling, choosing, and behaving contrary to God's truth.
For your faith and Scripture to be relevant, your challenge is to specifically identify your fleshly patterns, recognize when you are tempted to walk after the flesh, renounce that

Self-examination is not only examining what is true of your new self and declaring it, it is also examination—evaluation, assessment—of how well you are implementing spiritual truth:

- Where did I do well?
- Where did I fail?
- Where do I need to improve?
- What was my motive?

You examine these questions, not to improve upon truth or the condition of your new self—both impossibilities—but to accurately assess truth and evaluate your practice of what is true. Notice the overlap here with the practice of reflection.

Because you are complete and fully accepted by God given your redemption by Jesus, you are free to honestly assess your performance: *Does my performance align with, and is it reflective of, what God says is true of Him and me?*

Your *acceptance* with God is secure and static whereas *approval* of your performance varies based upon the dynamic of your walk in the Spirit or after the flesh. Who you are and what you do are not the same thing.

You are accepted. Your performance may or may not be approved.

---

temptation, and set your mind on specific Scriptural truth that is the antidote to your specific temptation. Once you begin practicing what is true, a) you spend less time walking after what is not true, while b) creating new habit patterns for thinking, feeling, choosing, and behaving based upon what is true. In time, you will experience the habit patterns you hate weaken and the habit patterns for truth become more dominant and pervasive. In this way, you are transformed by the renewing of your mind (ref. Rom. 12:1-2). Take your time with the two worksheets. Ask your heavenly Father to guide you. If you need additional input, I've provided resources for you to investigate.

So when you confess that you are accepted in Christ Jesus, you are stating an irrevocable, unchangeable truth that exists in perpetuity.

When you reflect and assess your performance, you are evaluating motive, alignment, and outcome. While your identity is static, your ability to consistently reflect yourself accurately in what you do is dynamic.

When you confess a sin you've committed, you are declaring an incongruency between who you are and what you did. Your confession serves to help you clearly see what you did wrong, why you did wrong, and what you need to do to correct course.

But assessing performance alone can get tricky. So much about life is contingent upon others, unseen circumstances, and unknown variables. Outcomes are not always ideal, nor predictable, and success is not guaranteed even if you do everything right. While there is merit in evaluating actual performance, the purest form of evaluation examines motive.

Dallas Willard believed that attitude was more important than the discipline. Thus, what was your attitude, your disposition, as you entered the fray of today?

If your confession was, "Father, I'm depending on you," then regardless of outcome, God evaluates your performance as a success and approves. If your attitudinal disposition was one of independence, then regardless of quality of outcome, God evaluates your performance as failure.

Life is not about succeeding circumstantially. Life is about meeting each day, and every circumstance, trusting in the power of Christ in you to live through you. Regardless of outcome, this motive for living always meets with God's approval and is the definition of success.

The rigor of self-examination and confession work to sophisticate and deepen your application of truth. Confession and assessment define and clearly demarcate the line between your acceptance and the approval of your performance.

When you self-evaluate, you are not judging you. You are justified by Christ. Rather, self-assessment judges performance and either approves or disapproves, and if appropriate, determines steps for improvement.

Thus, this particular use of the spiritual practice of confession is a self-examination of what went wrong/right and why. It is verbal, or silent, or written—declarations that enforce, hold accountable, and that empower and inspire spiritual responsibility to sophisticate your comprehension of truth and sharpen your application.

Sextius, a Roman philosopher, wrote, "When the light has been removed and my wife has fallen silent, aware of this habit that's now mine, I examine my entire day and go back over what I've done and said, hiding nothing from myself, passing nothing by."

Scripture puts this practice of self-assessment—the practice of confession—this way: "We are destroying speculations and every lofty thing raised up against the knowledge of God, and we are taking every thought captive to the obedience of Christ."[143]

---

[143] 2 Corinthians 10:5.

Chapter five of Hebrews notes that Jesus "learned obedience" through the rigor of the suffering He endured.[144] Jesus knew who He was and why He came, but as a human being He practiced what was true during hardship and learned how His earthly obedience correlated with spiritual reality. In this way, He *confessed* with both His teaching and His life what relationship with God is and how that relationship is demonstrated.

The spiritual practice of confession is multi-faceted. Thus, the complexity and breadth of this chapter.

However, simply put, the spiritual practice of confession is the discipline of declaring in your soul what your spirit knows is true so that confusion is ferreted out of your spiritual walk and any incongruity between what you say, and believe, and do is resolved. The practice of confession facilitates your heart's desire and functional ability to put into action what you believe.

The embrace within your soul of what your spirit knows, and the physical demonstration of this in your life, not only satisfies your heart's desire but is the confession of your life.

---

[144] Cf.: Hebrews 5:8.

Questions and Considerations

1. It is stated in this chapter, "Repetitive discipline—that is, diligent and determined practice—engages the spiritual fundamentals with enough frequency and duration of time to transform your habitual ways of thinking, feeling, and deciding to behave to better reflect what is true." What of your habitual ways—what the Bible calls flesh—bother you most? What spiritual habits would you like to see replace the fleshly habits that bother you? Can you integrate what you know from exercising the spiritual practice of reading the Bible, considering Scripture utilizing the spiritual practice of reflection, and implementing the spiritual practice of confession, i.e., here is a habitual way that is not my heart's desire, compared to a biblical reality that is my heart's desire, and here's what setting my mind of a true confession looks like?

2. This chapter describes a confession not only as something true, but as something declared. Why do you believe a personal declaration—a confession of belief— is of critical importance?

3. As this chapter concludes, there is a correlation made between self-examination and the attitude with which this evaluative process is engaged. With the confession

of self-examination, what are you actually evaluating? The chapter would say you are examining and then confessing whether or not your performance and motive align with your true identity and desire to walk in the Spirit. What do you think? Finally, the chapter suggests that if your self feels threat, your attitude will be defensive, but if your self is secure and it is your performance that is being evaluated, your attitude is anchored in security. Your thoughts on this?

EIGHT

The Spiritual Practice
of Submission

> **"**
>
> *"The essence of sin is arrogance. The essence of salvation*
>
> *is submission."*
>
> *Alan Redpath*

I'm a child of the tumultuous 60s and 70s. Resentment. Rebellion. Revolution. Rock 'n roll!

Our disillusionment collided with approval by the FDA of "the Pill" in 1960 and a sexual revolution was born. Free love. Free sex. An explosion of sexually transmitted diseases and the right to commit abortion in 1973 lest our freedom create an obligation.

Men had few bearings upon which to draw to guide their masculine identity. Their role models were the Great Generation (1901-1927) who'd won WW II, but who didn't tell their stories. Wedged in between the Great Generation and my generation, the Boomers (1946-1964), were those of the Silent Generation, born between 1928 and 1945. They were called the silent generation for a reason.

As the men of the 60s and 70s wandered in search of their masculine soul, women redefined their roles. They eyed the housewife role of their mothers and the submission taught by the church and revolted. The women's revolution. Feminism. Burned bras. A woman can do anything a man can do.

Powerful women. Weak men. The push for equality—not defined as equal in value, but as same in ability—has now progressed to pondering whether or not men are even necessary.

John Launer, Associate Dean of postgraduate medical education at the University of London, believes that men's future as part of the human species is terminal. He bases his reasoning upon the forty-or-so species where the female kills the male either before or after copulation. Considering the human male's propensities toward violence, not being as physically hearty as females, and doing worse scholastically than women, the good doc concludes, "The purpose of males has instead become one of the biggest unanswered questions in science."[145]

Tanya Gold writes, "Scientists have used embryonic stem cells to make synthetic sperm. My first thought is - does it come in pink? But the possibility grows (and I'm wilfully (sic) hopping and skipping and bouncing over the science bit here) that we will at some vague point in the future be able to breed without men." As she wonders whether a world without men would be problematic, Ms. Gold examines "the history of men" based upon war, leadership, religion, the environment, psychiatry,

---

[145] Launer, Dr. John. "Do We Even Need Men?" *Lithub.com*. April 24, 2018. https://lithub.com/do-we-even-need-men/

music, literature—noting that all great literature is "written by the losers in life"—and cinema.

Her article concludes that "men are the cause of all things terrible in the world," but since she would miss having sex with them, she will simply "...fantasise (sic) about this sweet new world" she envisions of a world without men.[146]

Lest you think this a recent notion—that men are unnecessary—recall Gloria Steinem's famous quip, "A woman needs a man like a fish needs a bicycle." In actuality, she was quoting Irina Dunn from 1970.

Responding to a congratulatory note from *Time* magazine about her recent marriage—ironically—Ms. Steinem set the record straight: "In fact, Irina Dunn, a distinguished Australian educator, journalist and politician, coined the phrase back in 1970 when she was a student at the University of Sydney. She paraphrased the philosopher who said, 'Man needs God like a fish needs a bicycle.'"[147]

It's a truism: If you listen to a person long enough, they will eventually tell you what's really on their mind. Ms. Dunn does this for us. In her response to Gloria Steinem's recognition, she correlates the rationale undergirding her feminism to her view of God.[148]

---

[146] Gold, Tanya. "Would a World Without Men Be Really So Bad?" *TheGuardian.com*. July 8, 2009. https://www.theguardian.com/lifeandstyle/2009/jul/09/women-men-better-off-without

[147] Editors. "The meaning and origin of the expression: A woman needs a man like a fish needs a bicycle." *Phrases.org*. Accessed, 18 December 2021. https://www.phrases.org.uk/meanings/a-woman-needs-a-man-like-a-fish-needs-a-bicycle.html

[148] Ibid.

Although she didn't realize she was doing so in 1970, Ms. Dunn sets the table for our examination of the spiritual practice of submission.

Talk of submission is repressive. Religious input advancing submission as biblical and godly is intemperate, offensive, degrading, disrespectful, and an affront to women. Besides, submission is a prop for men too weak to justify their existence.

In the battle of the sexes, there's no room for mercy. Only the weak yield or submit.

Is the practice of submission outdated (along with the Bible), inappropriate, irrelevant?

Is it possible that submission means something different than subservient, lesser, unequal, unqualified, relegated to another's dominance, especially another so deeply flawed that science questions male existence as viable?

Is it possible that submission is positive not punitive?

Possible, but seemingly unlikely given the oft-cited biblical directive: "Wives, be subject to your husbands, as is fitting in the Lord."[149]

What this verse and its companion passages mean in a popular culture morphing by the day is tricky business, but that's why I'm writing. Just because the merits of submission are obscured, misunderstood, or doubted doesn't mean the practice is not fundamental to our wellbeing.

---

[149] Ephesians 5:22.

Since this verse from Ephesians is like the elephant in the room when the topic of submission is broached, let's start with what the verse does *not mean* and work our way backward.

It is not only unreasonable, it is unconscionable to assert that God is disrespectful toward women, or that He favors men over women. It is ludicrous to assert that this passage from the Book of Ephesians means men are superior, women inferior; men capable, and women incapable.

Neither is it possible that this passage is advocating for subservience. The Gospel of Christ frees us—men and women alike—from subservience to sin.[150] In Christ, we are endowed—richly blessed—with salvation, freedom, establishment, and are bequeathed with ultimate worth. It's not biblically rational nor logically consistent to assert that women are freed through the Gospel from subservience to sin only to become subservient to men.

Subservience indicates a flawed relationship, for both the one who is servile and the one who dominates. Inequality has no place in either the human or divine realm.

The creation story reports that with each phase of creation, God pronounces His endeavors "good." However, when he makes Adam and places him in the garden, He observes him and says, "It is not good for the man to be alone. I will make him a helper corresponding to him."[151] The story goes on to report that God caused a deep sleep to come over Adam. While he was "under," God extracted one of his ribs and

---

[150] Cf.: Romans 8:1-2 and Galatians 3:23-29.
[151] Genesis 2:18.

fashioned—literally: He "built"—a woman and brought her to Adam.[152]

The storyline brings to my mind the image of the yin-yang circle.[153]

Without both parts, the image doesn't work. Put both parts together and they form a circle. They complement, they correspond, they fit together to form a whole, an entirety, a unity, a one.

It's as though the Genesis story is implying God's process of human creation being so remarkable, so profound, and so incredible that it took God two tries—perhaps a better wording would be, two steps—to get mankind like He wanted us to be: a male-female complimentary package that is created in His image and designed to reflect His image.

Favoritism, capriciousness, and punitive behavior are the stuff of insecure individuals. God is many things, but He is neither insecure nor petty and He has no favorites. Jesus Christ proves this and dispels any notion of God existing outside the realm of pure, absolute, unqualified love.

---

[152] Genesis 2:21-22.

[153] Yes, I'm aware that the image comes from Chinese philosophy. This doesn't make the image or what it conveys pagan or wrong. It means that God gave some ancient Chinese folks understanding about how complimentary systems function. Cf.: Proverbs 21:30 and James 1:17.

God is SO complete, and so utterly perfect, that as it turns out, when He created mankind in His image it wasn't possible to do so in either a male or a female. To accurately convey Himself, God determined He needed two sorts of humans, both of whom He called man.

Reflecting on creation, Genesis reports, "This is the book of the generations of Adam. In the day when God created man, He made him in the likeness of God. He created them male and female, and He blessed them and named them Man in the day when they were created."[154]

God made a male man and a female man. He blessed both equally as one being while endowing each with unique roles and abilities. Thus, both men and women are tasked with reflecting aspects of God that the other gender can't demonstrate—yet need demonstrated for them by their gender opposite to have any chance of more-fully conceptualizing God.

It is shortsighted to say a woman's place is in the home. It is also shortsighted to declare that all men are leaders, or that all men are good decision-makers, or that all men are wise guides. Building a box for men and a box for women is akin to building a box for God. It can't be done!

Deriving a definition of submission based upon gender or roles is narrow enough to be unreliable, but defining submission by traditional gender roles in Western culture is what we've done. In so doing we've recoiled at the concept of submission as defined by culture and missed the practice of submission as a spiritual discipline. Never mind

---

[154] Genesis 5:1-2.

that in so doing we've also diminished the remarkability of all concerned: men, women, and most of all, God.

"All the spiritual disciplines have the potential to become destructive if misused," writes Foster, "but submission is especially susceptible to this problem. As a result, we need to be clear regarding its limits. The limits of the discipline of submission are at the points at which it becomes destructive. It then becomes a denial of the law of love as taught by Jesus and is an affront to genuine Christian submission."[155]

Before launching into his thoughts on submission in Ephesians 5, Paul writes, "...and be subject to one another in the fear of Christ."[156] Then he develops what he means by being subject to one another: wives to your husbands, the church to Christ, children to parents, and husbands to their wives by loving them as Christ loves.[157]

There are distinct roles men and women play in their relationships. While no marriage is like the other in daily dynamic, every Christian marriage has the same foundation as reflected in the traditional marriage vows: to love and cherish until death do you part.

Said another way, marriage is given to us by God not only to procreate and populate the earth, but to pantomime[158] in our earthly marriages the spiritual marriage between God and the church. Just as God gives us friends to help us comprehend what it means to be a friend of God, and gives

---

[155] Foster, Richard. "Understanding Submission." *Renovare.org*. October 2014. https://renovare.org/articles/understanding-submission
[156] Ephesians 5:21.
[157] Ephesians 5:21ff.
[158] Pantomime: The telling of a story without words, by means of bodily movements, gestures, and facial expressions. *The American Heritage Dictionary,* 5th Edition.

THE SPIRITUAL PRACTICE OF SUBMISSION

us family to help us understand the magic of being in the family of God, so God gives us marriage to portray what He means when He declares us, the church, His bride.[159]

When a man and woman pledge themselves in marriage, they pledge to love one another throughout all the challenges of life. The vows taken are not self-serving, they are self-sacrificing. To love as Christ loves is to submit ourselves to a life of service, care, unconditional love, and self-denial.

Did you notice the definition I just created for biblical submission?

The spiritual practice of submission is the spiritual practice of loving as Christ loves, not only in marriage, but in all aspects of life. Living in this manner is an affront to pride and self-preservation. Yielding up ourselves as superior, or better, or preferred, or entitled sabotages the faux strength of self-sufficiency and the faux power of self-establishment and places us in position to understand that our lives are in Christ alone.

Thus, the obedient practice of submission brings to light true strength and power. From your position of security within the heart of God, the contrast between earthly and spiritual strength and power is stark. The practice and discipline of submission then serves to align your understanding of strength and power with God's perspective.

This lifestyle and attitude are contrary to culture. Spiritual submission is challenging—so challenging, in fact, that

---

[159] Cf.: Ephesians 5:22-33, esp. v. 32.

adopting this attitude of mind requires practice to understand, appropriate, and maintain.

Richard Foster says,

> The touchstone for the Christian understanding of submission is Jesus's astonishing statement, 'If any want to become my followers, let them deny themselves and take up their cross and follow me (Mark 8:34).' This call of Jesus to 'self-denial' is simply a way of coming to understand that we do not have to have our own way. It has nothing to do with self-contempt or self-hatred. It does not mean the loss of our identity or our individuality. It means quite simply the freedom to give way to others. It means to hold the interests of others above our own. It means freedom from self-pity and self-absorption.
>
> Indeed, self-denial is the only true path to self-fulfillment. To save our life is to lose it; to lose our life for Christ's sake is to save it (see Mark 8:35).[160]

Johnny Calhoun says, "The discipline of submission is the desire to have Jesus as the Master of my life in absolutely every way."[161] This desire is true—must be true—for both men and women because it is reflective of how we as human beings are designed to relate to God. Thus, the mutual submission we demonstrate to each other is intended to help us conceptualize, understand, and grasp in more nuanced ways how we relate to Jesus Christ and trust Him for all aspects of our lives.

---

[160] Foster. Ibid.

[161] Calhoun, Johnny. "The Spiritual Discipline of Submission." *Issuu.com*. Accessed, 10 December 2021. https://issuu.com/johnnycalhoun/docs/spiritual_disciplines_deeper_walk_b/s/75410

Marriage is simply the most common arena in which you practice the discipline of submission. In fact, as Calhoun stated above, practicing submission inside the entirety of your life serves your desire to have Christ edified in all aspects of your life. Not only this, but as you practice this discipline you portray as only you can do the magnificence of being the bride of Christ. Thus, whether married or single, practicing the discipline of submission facilitates your heart's desire to grasp what it means to be joined to God.

As you can see, the spiritual practice of submission is not demeaning but noble. Like the other disciplines, it is following the example of Christ's practices as He demonstrated His desire to submit to God in all ways.[162] Only secure, confident, strong, and truly powerful people can practice true and healthy submission.

Returning to "wives be subject to your husbands:" The passage is not elevating men and demeaning women. As I trust you now understand, this can't be the meaning of the verse.

Rather, the instruction is, a) offering women a resourceful focus that is advantageous to them in their quest to live godly lives, while b) equipping them to properly manage their power, in the context of c) pantomiming within marriage how Christ submitted to God.

Thus, women channel their power in order to demonstrate to themselves, their husbands, and onlookers how our submission as men and women in the Body of Christ is respectful of God. A picture is worth a thousand words—and without saying a word, this passage of Scripture positions women to lead men, other women, and children in

---

[162] Cf.: John 5:19 and 30.

portraying how the church compliments and corresponds to God.

Men's roles demonstrate one aspect of our relationship with God. Women's roles demonstrate another. Together, like diamonds showcased against a dark backdrop with a light shining through them, men and women showcase the many-faceted brilliance of new people who are in right relationship with God.

Of course, as noted earlier, all the spiritual disciplines can be abused and mismanaged. This is especially true for the practice of submission as Foster stated: "The limits of the discipline of submission are at the points at which it becomes destructive. It then becomes a denial of the law of love as taught by Jesus and is an affront to genuine Christian submission."[163]

I was speaking on the spiritual disciplines recently with a group of ministry leaders. Their pushback was strong! One accused me of "damnable and pernicious" heresy, others that I was teaching legalism, others that I was advocating that we walk after the flesh to improve our standing with God.

Let's be clear: There is nothing you can do, or fail to do, that will enhance, alter, diminish, change, or otherwise affect positively or negatively your acceptance by your heavenly Father. Regarding your worth, you are the pearl of great price Jesus spoke about.[164] As to heresy: baloney!

Note this summarized guidance from Philippians: "Do nothing from selfishness or empty conceit, but with

---

[163] Foster. Ibid.
[164] Cf.: Matthew 13:44-45.

humility of mind regard one another as more important than yourselves. Have this attitude in yourselves which was also in Christ Jesus, who, although He existed in the form of God, did not regard equality with God a thing to be grasped, but emptied Himself. He humbled Himself by becoming obedient."[165]

The essence of submission is comprised of humility, mindset, and attitude. This is true for both men and women, but the unique and individual roles men and women play demonstrate unique and individual aspects of humility, mindset, and attitude.

Love determines the most redemptive thing for another individual and then takes action. This is a sacrifice. By definition, love gives without thought of return. Love is humbling. Love is an act of self-sacrifice in order to create redemption in another.[166]

We are all tempted toward self-survival, selfishness, self-promotion, and self-determination. To live opposite of this self-centeredness requires adopting a mindset that opposes pride, position, and an attitude of self-importance. The conflict between self-significance and self-denial is the fundamental sin of humanity, the original sin in the Garden, and the constant that drives humanity to subdue and subjugate others in order to establish their own self-esteem and self-sustainability.

In a word, the most fundamental of all sins is pride. This is why Jesus' instruction is radical and counterintuitive: If you wish to have life, give up your life.[167]

---

[165] Philippians 2:1-9.

[166] Cf.: 1 Corinthians 13.

[167] Cf.: Matthew 16:25.

The harder it is to humbly submit yourself in a given situation is an indicator of how enticing the temptation is to forego submission of self and opt instead for self-elevation, self-aggrandizement, self-worth, and self-sufficiency.

This is why the spiritual discipline of submission requires practice.

Humility is hard—for both men and women.

A man wants to conquer, to best an opponent, to be victorious in the arena. If successful, he holds his head high, endows upon himself self-sufficiency, self-made man, and struts with cockiness. While winning is not bad, the temptation is to embrace the adulation as self-defining.

Pride is a potent intoxicant.

Just as it was tempting for Christ to embrace His divinity at the expense of His humanity, it is tempting for men to embrace their strength as defining and their successes as self-establishing. Just as Christ humbled Himself in obedience, so men are instructed to submit themselves by laying aside their lives in order to love sacrificially, humbly, and obediently—even if it costs them their lives.[168] This is a humble approach to living as opposed to the alternative of vain pride.

When a man flaunts his strength, his overstatement—his posing, stridency, posturing, self-aggrandizing, strutting, vaunting of himself—exposes weakness that terrifies him. His internal fear asserts that he is not masculine, not strong, and doesn't have what it takes to be a real man. For a man whose identity is tied to winning, losing declares he has lost

---

[168] Cf.: Ephesians 5:25-33.

his essence as a man. In the face of this fear, a masculine façade is constructed. This charade is an abuse of true, masculine strength and injects into all arenas of his life the toxicity of a masculine soul that is threatened and insecure.

The delusional disposition that Adam adopted in the Garden of Eden was that his life belonged to him. *I'm my own man*, was the temptation the first man received, adopted, and declared as preferential to being reliant upon God. In the Garden of Eden, the sin of the pride of life was on full display.

What the first man failed to do in the Garden of Eden, the last Man demonstrated in the Garden of Gethsemane and completed on the cross of Calvary.[169]

In Eden, Adam had the opportunity to give his life for another—to give his life for his wife, Eve. He chose instead to follow her lead, but.... Had he declined to share in the choosing of independence from God, opting instead to live in utter dependence and honest relationship with God, then he would have been in position to demonstrate the true strength a man possesses: to give his life for another. When the consequence of death was pronounced upon his wife, had Adam had his wits about him and remained focused as a complete man, he would have had the option of saying to God, "Sir, with all due respect to you, may I offer my life in exchange for Eve's? May I take her place so that she can live and have a chance at embracing redemption and reconciliation?"

But the progenitor of humanity failed—failed himself, failed his wife, and failed us. Clinging to the pride of his life and independence from God, Adam bequeathed to us—to all

---

[169] Cf.: Romans 5:12-19; 1 Corinthians 15:45-49.

humankind—the most fundamental, soul-sucking sins of all failings: pride of [perceived] life.

The last Adam, Jesus Christ, maintained His reliance upon God for each aspect of His life, thought, and belief.[170] And when the time came in Gethsemane, He was able to demonstrate true masculinity by laying down His life so others—you and I—might live, experience redemption, and enjoy reconciliation with God.

Jesus captured the true strength of self-submission, and demonstrated the gift men are uniquely designed to portray to their fellow human beings. He described this when He said, "Greater love has no one than this, that one lay down his life for his friends."[171] Similarly, "Whoever wishes to save his life will lose it, but whoever loses his life for My sake and the gospel's will save it."[172] Speaking of His role in the world and in our lives, He said, "I am the good shepherd; the good shepherd lays down His life for the sheep."[173]

The truly strong man lives a life of humble submission—submission to the confidence that his life is not his own but belongs to God. A strong man understands that by laying his life down for others, he pantomimes for us all how Jesus Christ lived.

Lest you misunderstand these lines about humility and submission to convey weakness of character and conduct, let me remind you that the One whom a man represents is the victorious warrior spoken of by Moses and Zephaniah, the lion depicted by Hosea, and the One who wages ultimate war as

---

[170] Cf.: John 5:19.
[171] John 15:13.
[172] Mark 8:35.
[173] John 10:11.

described by John the Revelator.[174] A man filled with the Spirit of God has the peace of Christ living within, but make no mistake: A godly man is still the exemplar of God's justice when called upon. He's just clear about true strength and true victory.[175]

Thinking again about the instruction in Ephesians for women to submit to their husbands, Lewis writes in *The Four Loves*, "The husband is the head of the wife just in so far as he is to her what Christ is to the Church. He is to love her as Christ loved the Church—read on—*and give his life for her.*" Lewis goes on to point out that the crowning of man as head of the home is done with a crown of thorns and that this headship "...is most fully embodied not in the husband we should all wish to be but in him whose marriage is most like a crucifixion."[176]

When He thought of a man, God's intent was that a man might live in such a manner that others would see a portrait of Him and be drawn to salvation. Practicing the discipline of submission guards a man against the delusion of culture, the pride of life, and the strength he possesses. Practicing the discipline of submission assists a man in staying focused on why he lives, how he lives, and for what purpose.

If men are strong, women are powerful.

I've never understood feminism's aspiration for women to be like men. What could be more demeaning and less edifying? How is femininity established by adopting masculinity as preferable? Besides, no matter the narrative, a woman will never be a man. Why would she want to be— unless her perception of femininity is shipwrecked?

---

[174] Cf.: Exodus 15:3, Zephaniah 3:17; Hosea 5:14; Revelation 19:11ff.

[175] Cf.: Psalm 33:13-22.

[176] Lewis, C.S. *The Four Loves.* Harcourt, Brace, and Company. New York, NY. 1960.

Reflecting again on Gloria Steinem and Irina Dunn: In one sense, these women are correct. Apart from being handy to have around when a jar needs opening, men are more and more relegated to mere sperm donors, and if people like Tanya Gold and John Launer have their way, synthetic sperm will be readily available, offered in pink, with no doubt a recipe of desirable y-characteristics, and men as a humanoid species can be dispensed with altogether.

Women possess powerful mojo. So powerful, that a woman's temptation to abuse her power can make her susceptible to becoming self-sustaining, self-sufficient, self-imposing, self-righteous, and self-ruling. So powerful is femininity that a woman can kill with a smile, and wound with her eyes. The power of a woman need never give in. She can simply change her mind and leave you grasping at her shadow. She can do as she pleases. She's nobody's fool.[177]

Power is intoxicating, enticing—even corrupting. An abuse of power is a shadow of what is true. Pride: I don't need anyone, including a man.

If a man's temptation is that he is strong enough to conquer, to win, and to establish himself ruler of his domain and captain of his soul, then a woman's temptation is to wield such power as to not need God any more than she needs a man.

As it turns out, in her feminism as a powerful woman, Ms. Dunn was correct about the underlying driver for feminine power: "A [female] man needs God like a fish needs a

---

[177] Cf.: Joel, Billy. "Always a Woman Lyrics." *Lyrics.com*. STANDS4 LLC, 2021. Web. 13 Dec. 2021. https://www.lyrics.com/lyric/14955620/Billy+Joel. The song reached #17 on the pop music charts.

bicycle." Such is the tempting allure of power as only women possess it.

It's interesting that the Bible doesn't instruct a wife to love her husband. Rather, it states, "...let the wife see to it that she respects her husband."[178] The humility of bestowing respect, especially as a powerful person, is a remarkable trust.

Just as it was tempting for Christ to cling to the power of His divinity, it can be tempting for a woman to cling to her power as a woman.

Pride is enticing for us all. Self-importance. Self-worth. Self-establishment, by me, for me, apart from everyone else—including God.

Men are strong. Women are powerful. The spiritual practice of submission is designed to help each manage their most profound temptations in order to appropriately portray our relationship with God in pantomime.

The practice of submission is an adoption of attitude, a setting of the mind, a relinquishing of self-determination, an active embrace of sacrifice on behalf of another. The discipline is the regular doing. The practice of the discipline creates sophistication.

The practice of submission actively combats our vulnerability toward pride.

Ah, the original temptation by the serpent in the Garden: "Eat this and you will be like God."[179] Pride. Once the

---

[178] Ephesians 5:33.
[179] Genesis 3:5.

forbidden fruit was eaten and the first humans became gods, they seized upon their self-established pride and girded themselves with independence, far from God in the Land of Nod, east of Eden.[180]

Pride: the basic sin, the fundamental shortfall, the root, the cancer coursing through and consuming the old man, setting him up as god and intoxicating him with delusional notions that in his pride he is worthy to stand before God self-justified.

Any circumstance vulnerable to the temptations of self-elevation, self-importance, and self-will is the red flag marking pride's potential germination. As the most basic of all temptations, it is the temptation common to us all as human beings, the most tempting of all temptations, and the most flagrant of all sins because it notionally establishes us as gods, rivals to the true God.

Thus, the importance of practicing the spiritual discipline of submission.

In all ways, throughout every aspect of life, we practice love, humble ourselves, and see to other's wellbeing. As fellow travelers on the journey of life, men and women serve one another by submitting to each other—and in so doing, each demonstrates Christ as only they can do given the roles they perform. Thus, it is in giving up your life that you discover life.

We could explore the passage of Scripture that says, "Children, honor your parents." The admonition of the verse

---

[180] Genesis 4:16.

is for parents to teach their children humility and the practice of it as a necessary skill in life.

If we had time, we could discuss submitting to the government, authorities, unjust rulers, and slave masters.

Although it is important to reconcile injustices and social discord, the imperfections of living in this fallen world are first and foremost opportunities for us to practice the spiritual discipline of submission. Otherwise, we are prone to believe human systems, government chief among them, can establish us as people of worth, importance, and significance (think, Socialism). Or, that human systems can correct inequity (think, Communism).

Circumstances serve to assist you in your accountability to humility, your dependence upon Christ as your life, and do so while facilitating your resistance to pride's entitlement.

You are called to humility, just as your Older Brother chose to live. The practice of submission serves this spiritual discipline.

Have this attitude which Christ demonstrated: Do not think yourself superior. Humble yourself as a matter of practice. Discipline your understanding of life in Christ. In so doing, you guard your heart against pride.[181]

While counterintuitive, it is in humbling yourself— submitting yourself—that you love, live, and discover personal fulfillment. Thus, in practicing the spiritual discipline of submission, you learn the beauty of how Christ lived.

---

[181] Cf.: Proverbs 4:23.

In practicing the spiritual discipline of submission, you discover freedom, just as the quote by Aristotle at the beginning of the book declared: "Through discipline comes freedom."

Questions and Considerations

1. The thesis of this chapter is that submission is positive, not punitive—for both men and women. Your thoughts regarding why this is important in a consideration of the spiritual practice of submission?

2. The default definition of submission has to do with power and hierarchy. However, this chapter presents submission as the desire to have Jesus as master of your life in absolutely every way. Assuming this an accurate and biblical definition of submission, how does this change your concept of submission and inform your practice of this spiritual discipline?

3. The practice of submission is a direct assault on the sin of pride in a quest to establish humility within your soul. Given that pride is one of the seven deadly sins, if not the root of all sin, then the importance of submission as a devoted practice is made clear. Since this is the case Scripture is making, how does this guide, adjust, alter, inform, and clarify your practice of submission as a man? As a woman? As a single person, a married person, a leader, an employee, a minister, a parent, a child—whatever your position in life?

NINE

The Spiritual Practice
of Fasting

On March 19, 1982 I stood up from the lunch table and my back spasmed. The pain was excruciating as the spasms twisted and bent my spine against its design specifications.

With previous episodes, the spasms abated after a few days. But as time passed, this occurrence was different: The spasms persisted and became chronic.

Incessant pain is a powerful motivation.

As time dragged on, I became more and more desperate for relief. I saw a plethora of doctors and practitioners who performed numerous tests, prescribed various treatments, and offered little in the way of a diagnosis. Nothing worked worth noting.

My options for healing were getting slim. I needed God to intervene, to heal, to reinstate my physical equilibrium.

So, I prayed. And I prayed. And I asked others to pray. I prayed through a list. I prayed for others so I would not appear selfish. I prayed lying down. I prayed kneeling down. I prayed naked, I prayed clothed. I prayed impromptu and I prayed in Jesus' name.

Nothing. As Lewis observed, "Go to Him when your need is desperate, when all other help is vain, and what do you find? A door slammed in your face, and a sound of bolting and double bolting on the inside. After that, silence."[182]

I needed help. Real help. I couldn't sleep, couldn't sit, couldn't stand, couldn't find anything to ease my discomfort.

Desperate times require desperate measures.

There was nothing left to do but go on a fast. You know, get God's attention.

For forty days, I fasted. It was a food fast of biblical proportion.

Mr. Gore had not yet invented the internet, so research about fasting was not at my fingertips. In my addled state it didn't occur to me to read anything on the subject. Fasting was in the Bible. The men and women of the faith fasted. Jesus fasted. If it worked for them, it would work for me. I hoped.

---

[182] Lewis, C.S. *A Grief Observed*. HarperOne. New York, NY. 2009.

As I write to you, I've endured the pain that began on that March day in 1982 every moment of every day since. On a good day, when I lie down at night there are about twenty seconds of blessed relief. On a bad day....

In retrospect, I didn't go on a fast all those years ago. I went on a hunger strike.

But fast, hunger strike. Whatever.

Fasting didn't work. Yet, any list of the spiritual disciplines includes the practice of fasting.

Why?

First, as I've come to realize, fasting is not a hunger strike to get God's attention, for the simple reason that God doesn't need His attention gotten. He knows all. He never sleeps, doesn't even doze. He knows the number of hairs on your head and considers you the apple of His eye. He loves you without reservation, is dedicated to your wellbeing, and promises His faithfulness, goodness, and lovingkindness to you all the days of your life. He knows you—knows everything about you. He wants the best for you. You don't need to get His attention.

Second, to approach fasting as a means to gain God's favor, impress Him, improve your standing with Him, or to convince Him you are serious, godly, or more dedicated than ever before to living a spiritual life is a misuse of the practice of fasting. Your standing with God is based upon one thing: whether or not you are in Christ.

Either you are or you aren't—in Christ Jesus.

If not, then you are outside of God, apart from His life, and not included in the family of God. If you are a Christian, a Believer, a person who has accepted God's salvation by faith alone in Christ alone, then you are in Christ.

You are close. You are indwelt, sealed, and double-secured in Christ, in God.[183] You are endowed with a new identity, set apart for God, forgiven, justified, and redeemed. Everything that separated you from God has been reconciled. Nothing stands between you and Him. The person who is in Christ is as close to God as Christ Himself. Nothing can enhance this position you have. Nothing can diminish it either.

If you are in Christ, you are close.

If you are not in Christ, then you are far away.

So, why are you supposed to practice the spiritual disciplines if your standing with God is secured and complete?

The obvious answer is that the spiritual disciplines are not intended to restore, enhance, or otherwise amend your standing with God. Therefore, practicing the disciplines of the faith must be for another purpose.

Candidly, you cannot do, perform, or enact any behavior that will improve who God has already declared you to be as a result of being included in the life of Jesus Christ. Throughout the New Testament, but especially the Book of Hebrews, Scripture references the work of Christ as

---

[183] Cf.: John 14:20. For anything to get to you, it must first pass through God, through Jesus, to get to you—and when it gets to you, it finds you filled with Jesus, indwelt by the Holy Spirit of God.

finished, complete, and entirely fulfilling of God's standards. Thus, if you are in Christ, then you are complete in Him.[184]

This is an amazing thing! No matter how we may try, I seriously doubt our earth-bound selves will ever comprehend more than a smidgen of God's magnificent grace and mercy.

Yet, we know God's mercy and grace are there. We know they are true. We comprehend that we are the beneficiaries of His lovingkindness toward us.

But the fog of our humanity, the noise of life, the residuals of the Fall, the bumping grinding of (fill in the blank) renders a chasm, almost a schism, between what we know spiritually and what we think about, feel, and the choices we must make inside our souls. It feels at times as though our spirits live in one world and our souls in another. It feels as though our spirit speaks one language and our soul another.

Yet, this cannot be true! A new person in Christ cannot in functional reality be partially new and partially old as some assert. The old self cannot be partially dead, positionally dead, or in its dying throes until physical death finally releases us from the old self's rebellions. Either Christ accomplished salvation or He did not.[185]

---

[184] Cf.: Hebrews 10:1-25; Colossians 2:8-14.

[185] The question is: Why do you sin as a Christian? You want to please God, but often do the very things you hate. Why? Note, this is the same question posed in Romans 7:15 and its larger context of, 7:7-25.

The simplistic—and incorrect—answer to the question is that the declaration of Romans 6:6 (Cf.: 6:1-11) about the old self being crucified with Christ and a new self being raised with Christ is not functionally true. Rather, this is a positional truth—meaning, it's the position God takes and is true in His mind but it's not applicable for you during your earthly life. So, given this line of reasoning, when will you functionally be freed from your

We are new creations in Christ... who contend with duplicity, intrigue, impurity, and conflict inside our souls—

old self? When you die and go to heaven. This is the reasoning underlying the theology of those who answer the question by asserting that the old self remains alive.

But note the gravity of the problems with the explanation above: 1) The grammar of Romans 6:1-11 is past tense, not future tense for when you die someday. 2) For the final death of the old self to occur at your physical death means that physical death accomplishes on your behalf something–the death of your old self and forgiveness for your sinfulness as a descendant of Adam (Cf.: Romans 5:12-21)–that Jesus Christ's death on the cross failed to accomplish. Thus, if the above reasoning is substantively accurate, then Jesus doesn't set you free from sin and death, physical death does. Salvation does you no good in this life, only in the next. Thus, a passage like Romans 8:2–"...Jesus Christ has set you free from the law of sin and death"–is not true today beyond theory.

The question still remains, but it is answered: Romans 5:12-8:2 explains the problem, the solution, and the functional application.

Romans 5:12-21 explains that God had two problems with you: 1) The sins you've committed, i.e., the rebellious, independent behaviors you perform; and 2) the fact that you are by birth, identity, and genetic disposition sinful as a result of being a descendant of Adam, the first man. This identity, termed the "old self" in Romans 6, is inherently sinful by nature, rebellious, darkened, and dead to God.

Romans 6:1-11 explains how God solved both of His problems with you. By the shed blood of Jesus, He forgave your sins, i.e., the things you do wrong that fall short of God's ideal. But also, by identifying your old self with the crucifixion, death, and burial of Jesus Christ, God effectively kills your old, Adamic, rebellious self. Then, in the resurrection of Christ, God raises up a new self, endowed with a new identity declared by God, and possessed of a new heart that desires the same things your heavenly Father's (God) heart desires. Thus, the old you is crucified with Christ and the new you, the new creation, is raised in Christ (Cf.: 2 Cor. 5:17; Galatians 2:20) and is alive to God.

Romans 7:6-25 explains that when the new self is tempted to sin, i.e., to perform as though the old self did not die in Christ, the temptation is not coming from within you but is in fact originating from the law of sin. In this passage, note that the use of the word "sin" is not verbal; rather, sin is a noun throughout the passage. The deceptive nature of how sin submits temptation for your–the new self–consideration is that he does so sounding like you, i.e., sounding like the old, dead self. Note that temptation is verbalized using first-person pronouns.

Romans 8:1-2 explains that the thesis of Romans 5:12-7:25 is true: The old self is dead, the new self is alive, and your new heart remains. Thus, there is no condemnation for you as a Believer. When you behave contrary to your true condition as a new person, it is because you are deceived. In your deception, you choose to live hypocritically–contrary to what is true of you and what is in your heart to do. The point is, temptation does not originate in you, as it once did when your old self was alive, but rather comes to you, the new person, from outside via the law of sin/sin/or the principle of sin.

To examine this in Scripture, you MUST use a reliable translation like *The New American Standard* Bible or the *English Standard Version*. The *New International Version* is a very poor translation and will only confuse you.

a daily contention to trust, to believe, and to walk in the Spirit; a frequent challenge to assess if our transformation is true and Christ is sufficient. Day in, day out, often moment-by-moment, our redeemed souls contend with the darkness asserting [against the truth and in vain] that who we are and whose we are is debatable, negotiable, or changeable.

This felt incongruity is where the spiritual discipline of fasting comes into play.

The McKays write, "Fasting is the most concrete and viscerally embodied of the spiritual disciplines, and its intersection of the physical and the metaphysical (i.e., spiritual) produces uniquely potent, perceptible, senses-arousing effects that bridge the often too-wide gap between body and soul."[186]

The McKays and I are not defining the components of our humanity in the same way, but we are saying the same thing: Often, given all the distractions and demands of life, a gap emerges between your spiritual life and your earthly life that renders your spiritual reality seemingly irrelevant to your earthly reality. You know this irrelevance must not be the actual case, but bridging the chasm is daunting.

One reason for this book is the widespread criticism that the church and her message are irrelevant—not applicable or useful—to life. Since the Gospel cannot be irrelevant, the fundamental problem must be how the truth of the Gospel is presented and practiced. Thus, our examination of the fundamental, basic disciplines of the faith.

---

[186] McKay, Brett and Kate. "The Spiritual Disciplines: Fasting." *ArtofManliness.com.* Accessed, 17 December 2021. https://www.artofmanliness.com/character/behavior/spiritual-disciplines-fasting/

Fasting creates leverage, acts like a bridge, and provides the incentive necessary to seize the day, gain momentum, or produce the clarity your faith needs to take the next step of trust. The discipline of fasting, like any form of discipline, produces congruity—synthesis—between your spirit, soul, and body. Recall the quote from Plato to open the chapter: "I fast for greater physical and mental efficiency."

The practice of fasting does not change your standing with God, but by engaging in a viscerally demanding activity while focusing on a spiritual truth, the practice of fasting facilitates the aligning of your soul with your spirit through physical demand. This alignment is not only indicative of your heart's true desire, the rigor of the practice eventuates the fulfillment of your heart's desire. Hebrews puts it like this: "All discipline for the moment seems not to be joyful, but sorrowful; yet to those who have been trained by it, afterwards it yields the peaceful fruit of righteousness."[187]

Virtually all religions teach the practice of fasting—for different reasons and motivations, obviously, but the point is: In your quest to fill the God-shaped vacuum designed into you, you recognize a chasm between this life and God's life. Even though complete in Christ, as Christianity teaches, there remains the struggle to align what you believe spiritually with what you live daily. By deliberately challenging your life with fasting, an intensity is created that facilitates congruence between spirit and soul, belief and behavior.

The most common fast is from food and/or drink. After missing a couple of meals, your attention is gotten. You are

---

[187] Hebrews 12:11.

hungry. Fasting from your favorite drink, or routine snack, or an aspect of your habitual diet garners your attention.

Once realized, you seize upon this heightened awareness, your discomfort, and use it to fuel the tenor of your prayer with a different intensity than is customary. This fast is not to get God's attention, as I illustrated earlier in my misguided zeal, but to focus your attention on how the Spirit of God is speaking to you, guiding you, and illuminating for you in your heightened sensitivity just how His perspectives may guide your earthly existence.

Using a fast to reset or recharge your physical health is great and something health counselors advocate, but to gain spiritually from a fast means that you make a determination to use the demands of fasting to focus your spiritual and soulical attention on a common objective: to meet with God in order to comprehend and understand to a greater degree the spiritual reality of your life in Christ and how this applies to and superintends your daily life.

The practice of fasting keeps you honest about what is true, what is truly in your heart, and what you truly need to live as God intends. Growth and change with this practice result in exchanging your habitual ways for God's ways.

Over the last weeks, I grew dissatisfied with how much time I was spending browsing Instagram. I was reading less, contemplating less... but I enjoyed Instagram and the images fed to me by its algorithms. I felt conflicted. I also felt weak, deprived, less vital.

Then my phone needed replacing—right before I departed for a demanding, week-long conference, followed immediately by a camping trip, followed shortly by an off-grid retreat.

The irregular schedule and funky access to the net were the incentives I needed.

When the new phone arrived, I booted it up with the simplicity of no Instagram app. I capitalized on a period of demanding and remote travel obligations to deny myself Instagram. The next sentence is critically important: And with the denial, i.e., the fast from Instagram, I determined to use the time gained to pray, to read Scripture, to journal, and to more clearly take inventory of how I wanted to spend my time while asking God for guidance on how He envisions me spending the time I have been granted.

Will I restart Instagram one of these days?

I don't know. That's TBD. For now, my denial is a fast from technology that is serving my spiritual purposes.

Over time, I've practiced fasting by living more simply. By this I mean, deliberately reducing the overhead of my earthly possessions to explore more earnestly God's provisions for me. At the same time, to more honestly consider the poor around me.

I've fasted for a time from forms of literature I enjoy to listen more intently to God via literature that transports my soul more reliably into the focus of my spirit. I've also fasted from simplistic Christian literature in order to digest Christian literature that demands more of me. I've fasted from types of music and volumes of music.

You can employ a fast with almost any aspect of life. The critical component of the fast is to discern and determine your intent in fasting.

Once again, you hear me identifying motive: What underlies the reason for your practice?

If there is a hint in your motive of performing a practice to gain favor with God, your practice is misguided. You are already favored by God because of the finished and completed work of Jesus Christ.

If your motive is to position yourself such that you hear more clearly, understand more deeply, and apply more consistently the spiritual reality that is yours upon your earthly life, then your motive is pure and your spiritual practice is working as intended.

You don't have to read your Bible and study. You don't have to journal and practice personal reflection. You don't have to practice confession, submission, fasting, or any other of the remaining spiritual disciplines.

Neither do you have to eat vegetables, exercise, get a good night's sleep, moderate your drinking, be diligent with your work, honor your word, hug your spouse and kids, manage time with your screens, or prioritize a family meal together.

But if you desire to get the most out of life and family, you will discipline your life such that you seize each day to your advantage.

Likewise, if you desire to more fully comprehend who God is, who He has declared you to be, and what it means that you are endowed with the presence of the Holy Spirit in your life, then you will put yourself in position to practice the disciplines of the faith.

Doing so puts you on the path your heart desires to walk— the place where God walks.

Questions and Considerations

1. The spiritual practices have a great deal to do with alignment, a clear perspective, a deep understanding of relationship between you and your heavenly Father and a clear-eyed examination of what misaligns, confuses, and perverts your heart's desire. Are you buying the thesis of this book to this point? What has convinced you, or in what aspects of the book's thesis are you questioning?

2. The spiritual discipline and practice of fasting is designed to increase awareness, create emotional, mental, and willful leverage toward realizing clarity, understanding, and heart's desire. What might a practice of fasting look like in your life to most effectively achieve the spiritual goals you are seeking to embrace?

3. Sound biblical doctrine teaches that your standing and relationship with God are based singularly upon the work of Jesus Christ. This means there is nothing left to achieve that Christ Jesus did not accomplish. But, oh my! It is so tempting to believe that what you do can enhance or detract from your position with God. Of all the spiritual practices, fasting is the most visceral, the most physical, tangible, and measurable. While the spiritual

practice of fasting heightens your awareness, it also makes you vulnerable to the belief that physical effort can change how God views you. So, how do you approach this discipline so that it works for you and not against your heart's desire?

TEN

The Spiritual Practice of Rest and Secrecy

There are many mysteries in the story of creation. One fascination is that after He had created all that He created, God looked around, considered His work, and took a break.

Genesis 2:2 says, "He rested on the seventh day from all His work which He had done."

The account goes on to say that as God rested, and contemplated His resting, He determined that taking a break from His labors was so important that He should sanctify—declare holy—the practice. Verse 3: "Then God blessed the seventh day and sanctified it, because in it He rested from all His work."

At first blush, it would appear that God was tired after working a six-day, work week. But that can't be. God doesn't get tired.

So what was so valuable, or important, about resting that it prompted God to call His day of rest holy? Why does the practice of rest rise to the level of being a spiritual discipline for us?

In your case, there is the obvious benefit of taking a break because you are physically, mentally, emotionally tired from your labors. Like Stanley Kubrick observed, "All work and no play make Jack a dull boy."

You can't lift weights or work out seven days a week and get stronger. Trying this will break your body. You need rest to promote recovery.

You can't burn the proverbial candle at both ends without either burning yourself or extinguishing your flame. Abusing your soul's work ethic, and suffering the consequence, isn't called burn-out without reason.

Work-a-holics may put in a lot of hours, but they do so by drawing down the reserves from elsewhere inside their souls. At some point, it will be time to pay the debt incurred. Further, a number of studies report that productivity drops if time is not taken to recharge, replenish, and restore.[188]

Perhaps no group of laborers is more stressed, burned out, or unproductive than ministers. Just because a person works in the vineyard of the Lord doesn't make them

---

[188] Cf.: Stevens, Samantha. "Vacation Days and Productivity in the U.S. versus Other Countries." *GlobalCallForwarding.com*. January 30, 2018.
https://www.globalcallforwarding.com/learn/vacation-days-productivity-u-s-vs-countries/

immune to fatigue. Stats indicate that 75% of ministers are extremely stressed. It's estimated that 80% of ministers will leave the profession within their first decade of work.[189] In her book, *Strengthening the Soul of Your Leadership*, Ruth Haley Barton writes to ministry leaders and says,

> Amid the welter of possible distractions, an essential discipline for leaders is to craft times of quiet in which we allow God to show us those things that we might otherwise miss. We need time for the chaos in our soul to settle so that we can turn aside to look at the great sights in our own life and seek understanding about what they mean.[190]

But physical wellbeing can't be the only benefit of rest. Something more is at play or God, who doesn't even need to sleep, would not have sanctified rest as important.

Another fascination with the creation story is that after each creation effort, God pronounced His work good. How could it not be? We're talking about God, and as the guy said, "God don't make no junk." But at the conclusion of His work week, upon reflection of all He had made, God said it was *very* good.

Good. Very good.

What's interesting is the qualitative analysis by God. All that He made is good, but upon closer examination, His evaluation improves to *very* good. The implication is that, a) His early work could have been better, b) His daily evaluation was inaccurate, or c) that in His rest God

---

[189] Gaultiere, Bill. "Pastor Stress Statistics." *SoulShepherding.org*. Accessed, 17 December 2021. https://www.soulshepherding.org/pastors-under-stress/

[190] Barton, Ruth Haley. *Strengthening the Soul of Your Leadership*. IVP Books. Downers Grove, IL. 2008.

demonstrates something essential to His wellbeing, an essential He derived during His rest.

An aspect of practicing rest is taking time to reflect.

Reflection has an element of evaluation. I will write more about this later, but my mentor taught me to take an extended time away to evaluate my year of work and make plans for the upcoming year. This reflection and evaluation have proven invaluable to my productivity and the quality of my work over the years.

Reflection also contains celebration—or should contain celebration; it certainly did for God, and we are created in His image.

I'm meeting with a group of men who are reading my book, *Swagger*. It was published about 15 months ago as of this writing. Apart from brief preparation prior to interviews, I haven't read the book since I published it. At the time of publication, I felt the book was good or I wouldn't have published it. But with a subsequent reading, two things are occurring: a) As is *always* the case, I'm finding miscellaneous edits (arrgghh!), and b) I'm pleased with what I wrote. There are chapters that are very good.

Upon reflection, I celebrate my work. I could celebrate in hopes of shoring up a sagging self-esteem that I'm a good writer, but this would be an abuse of my work and a dismissal of the fact that my self-worth is not in what I write but in what God declares to be true of me because I'm His son. I'm not what I do for a living. I'm who God says I am.

Because I'm confident in who I am based upon God's declaration of me, I'm free to approach my work without undue burden, i.e., requiring my labor as a writer to define me. Rather, as a secure man I'm free to celebrate my work for my work's sake.

But what if I review my work and realize I didn't do my best work? This is a real possibility. In fact, when I read some of my older writings, I think, *Yikes. I wish I hadn't written that like that.* What then?

Now we are back to motive and method, and here again, the rest of reflection reveals cause for celebration.

Let me illustrate: When I began writing this chapter, I worked my way through a standard routine getting started. One aspect of my start-up is that I open my document—blank in this case, but this routine also occurs when I'm editing my work—stare down at my keyboard, raise my hands into position but hovering two inches above the keys, and voice my determination. It goes like this, inside my head, in my thoughts: *Father, I'm answering your call to write. Please compose through me, grant me your ingenuity, and bless me with your words. I'm looking to you. Help me access my heart's desire.*

Then, I place my hands on the keyboard and begin typing my thoughts into the words that you are reading.

First, in praying this prayer I'm expressing my determination to rely upon the power of God's Spirit to write through me. This is what I believe it means to walk in the Spirit.

The alternative is to believe in my own skill, talent, and expertise as a writer. This is what I believe it means to walk after the flesh.

Second, I believe God honors and answers this prayer or I wouldn't pray it.

Thus, my determination is voiced and God's engaged in the process.

Now, back to whether what I write is good or not.

First: I *never* write a publishable first draft—of anything substantive. Not even an email. So, just because I write trusting the Spirit of God to guide me doesn't mean I write final first drafts. This means my trust in Christ, and my work, is a dynamic process not an outcome.

Second: Like I said, I believe my writing is good quality or I wouldn't publish it. However, my critics disagree. They believe I'm a hack, some think me a heretic, and others consider me boring, simplistic, a waste of time, unhelpful, and ignorant; I'm derided for being from the South, dense, old, white, conservative, not educated well enough, and I could go on.

Maybe I'm a good writer. Maybe not. Who's to say? Sales numbers are fickle. Readers love you for the last thing they liked. Publishers only want you if you have a personal list that buys books.

So when I come to my rest, how will I assess whether my work for the week was good and worthy of celebration?

Return to the paragraph containing the italic print conveying my prayer before I write: *Father, I'm looking to you.* This is the key.

While God is interested in my performance, He doesn't evaluate my success or failure based upon production, publication, quantity, quality, sales, accolades, or criticism. God evaluates whether my work is good or not based upon the motive-method I use to approach my work.

If I approach my work confident in my abilities as a writer, even if the critics love me and sales make me richer than the Queen, God will pronounce my work a failure because I produced it independently of Him and His Spirit through me.

If I approach my work confident in the power of the Spirit to write through me, then whether my work is praised or panned, upon reflection I can celebrate that my work was successful because I approached it relying upon the Spirit of God to write through me.

God's evaluation of work is based singularly upon whether I approached my duties in the power of the flesh—my ability, talent, expertise—or the power of the Spirit: *Father, I'm looking to you as I begin.*

Thus, when I rest after my labors and reflect, I am clear about what I'm celebrating and empowered to relinquish— to rest from—what is not part of success as defined by God. In this way, my rest is regenerative, restorative, replenishing, and fuels my recovery from a hard labor.

Of course, in a similar vein to my editorial process, I must add that I've got an entire bookshelf dedicated to books on writing that I've read and studied. I utilize an outside editor for everything substantive. I study my craft continually. I practice my craft diligently and am committed to excellence with every word I pen.

In other words, praying the prayer above and then throwing haphazard, ill-conceived, and less-than-the-best words onto the page is an affront to Christ, an abuse of my craft, disregard of my talent, and a disservice to you. I trust Christ, but I work at my craft really, really hard.

Trusting Christ for my writing and doing the work is a dance. As they say, "It takes two to Tango."

I can rest momentarily, and I do. I rest at the end of the day. But a day of rest is sanctified by God because it is of sufficient duration to restore me for what lies ahead tomorrow.

Hand-in-hand with rest is the spiritual practice of secrecy. As I rest and reflect and celebrate success, I practice secrecy—not broadcasting, announcing, sharing with others—as a means to resist the temptation to be recognized for what I've done as opposed to who I am.

There isn't anything wrong with being recognized.[191] In fact, when we fail to recognize the people around us, we make them vulnerable to Satan's accusation that they are not important and that their work doesn't matter. So, recognition is important—but it is not essential.

Recognition and significance are often used synonymously, but they are distinctly different concepts. While recognition is important and desirable, significance is essential.

As with all essentials—true needs—these are so important that God pledges to meet these needs Himself versus trusting others to supply these needs for us.[192] What Satan

---

[191] Cf.: Editors. "Spiritual Disciplines Index: Secrecy." *Renovare.org*. Accessed, 17 December 2021. https://renovare.org/articles/spiritual-disciplines-index-secrecy
[192] Cf.: Philippians 4:19.

does in an effort to deceive is to seize upon a lack of recognition and condemn us as not being significant.

It is one thing for my work to not be recognized. It is quite another to not be significant as a person.

In secrecy, because the moment is so sacred, I reflect during my rest upon my significance as a child of God. In so doing, I disarm the probability of connecting what I do—and any recognition received or withheld—as integral, important, or even related to my significance as a human being.

God alone establishes my significance. This status can neither be enhanced nor diminished. His valuation of me as significant is static, absolute, unimpeachable, unchangeable, and irrevocable because it is established by the completed, finished work of Christ and my position in Him.

Thus, in secrecy, I practice the spiritual discipline of resting to celebrate my labors as distinguished from my significance as a child of God. I rest in and I rest from—*in* my celebration and *from* the temptation to associate performance and recognition with personal significance.

During my rest, I celebrate my work. This is *good*. In secrecy, I celebrate that I'm significant because God has established this as true of me entirely apart from what I do for a living. This is *very good*.

The image of rest is often something to do with a lounge chair, few responsibilities, and fewer demands. Yes, well. This image is sketchy and hard to produce during an all-inclusive, child care provided, vacation on a cruise ship.

Life is a busy endeavor. Work six days and you've got a one-day weekend, much of which is consumed with Sunday activities. Work five days, you've got Saturday to take up slack.

Work fifty-sixty hours a week, commute to and from, attend your kids' activities, have friends for dinner; then, go to church for three hours Sunday morning, make it four-and-a-half if you go to lunch afterward, have small group Sunday evening and all but Saturday is blown out living life. But on Saturday you need to run errands, rake the yard, have family night, and on and on and on life spins.

You can see how important it is to properly define what you mean by rest. If rest is essential and rest means a lounge chair portside of a cruise ship, you are in trouble.

Rest can mean different than the norm. Rest can be something other than the thing you consider labor. Thus, mowing the grass can constitute rest (unless you run a lawn service). Same for doing the dishes, picking up the laundry, going to the grocery, and so forth. Rest can mean an altered pace

Personally, I define my labor as writing, as well as other keyboard demands like email and research. I'm also the chief cook, grocery shopper, and house manager. All of this, and the associated tasks, I labor to accomplish during my work week.

Then, I deliberately shift gears for the weekend. Unless I'm writing a book, which demands attention every day for months, I avoid my keyboard. I rarely go to the grocery on the weekend and I take time to make special meals for Friday or Saturday evening. My rest may include time in the garage, a longer walk, a yard project, sitting on the patio, and so forth. I read a different type literature during my rest since reading during the week is a required aspect of my labor.

While I'm moving and busy, I'm consciously thinking of the changed pace as rest. I am diligent to include time to reflect and to contrast my work week and my rest time.

Rest and secrecy overlap with other spiritual disciplines like silence, solitude, prayer, and friendship. More on these disciplines is upcoming.

Meanwhile, rest. You are filled with the Spirit and secure in Him. This is *good*. He has declared you to be significant. This is *very good*.

Thus, your labor matters to God. He wants to labor through you and wants to celebrate with you this collaboration. This is *good*.

You are significant. Hold to this secretly in your heart as it will protect you when recognition is out of balance. This is *very good*.

Questions and Considerations

1. Why do you believe God rested on the seventh day? This chapter asserts that the same practice is important for you? Agree or disagree? If so, then from whom do you hear, "Very good?"

2. Why is the process I describe as I prepare to write important to my discipline of rest? How can you generalize from the prayer I pray as a writer to whatever it is that you do in life? Why does this constitute the discipline of rest?

3. The discipline of secrecy insists upon distinguishing between public recognition and the private confidence that you are significant. How are you recognized in life? What makes you significant? How does one inform the other—or do they?

ELEVEN

The Spiritual Practice
of Silence

> **"**
>
> *"In silence God ceases to be an object*
> *and becomes an experience."*
> Thomas Merton

Silence. Quiet. Without noise. Without talk. Without the mental work of thinking. Silence. Not doing anything assertive beyond determining to be silent.

Henri Nouwen likens his quest to create silence as removing the scaffolding from his life. All distractions, interruptions, concerns, relational obligations, and demands that service the overhead of life, he distances himself from. In so doing, he rests upon the basis of his faith, identity, and theology: his relationship with God and God's relationship with him.

But why? What's important about silence—so important that it is classed among the spiritual disciplines?

Dallas Willard believes the spiritual practices of solitude and silence are the most important disciplines for

Christians today, especially pastors.[193] My personal experience confirms this view.

Many who write about the spiritual disciplines put the practice of solitude and silence together. I was tempted to do the same—but determined the practice of silence too important to share the same chapter with solitude. The two disciplines overlap, but each merits its own examination.

Silence, like the other disciplines of the faith, places you in position to interact with God. All of the disciplines are designed to assist your heart's desire to understand who God is and who you are, but each has its unique advantage to guide your journey of faith. In practicing silence, this discipline serves your heart's desire by establishing a quiet, intimate place to meet with God.

Nothing is quite so indicative of closeness like being quiet in the presence of someone else. Only the closest of friends are confident enough in their friendship to risk silence— risk because silence and intimacy go hand-in-hand.

"An intimate relationship need not be chock-full of constant conversation and noise," I wrote in a 1976 article.

The quiet of reading together or working together or being in the same house together is a form of quietness, but it's not true silence. When you are reading or working there is noise in your head. You are active thinking, calculating, pondering, planning, learning.

---

[193] Cf.: Gaultiere, Bill. "Solitude and Silence." *SoulShepherding.org*. Accessed, 18 December 2021. https://www.soulshepherding.org/solitude-and-silence/

Silence is nothing. Silence is neutral. Silence is intimate. Silence is being present without pretense or plan. This makes silence a place of vulnerability.

At night, I go for a walk in my neighborhood. I wait until dark. I typically don't wear my glasses, which I need to see distance. I don't walk with ear buds and I'm late enough that no one will call on the phone, which I only carry in case I need help.

Most people, frequently *all* my neighbors, are locked away in their houses when I step outside to walk. So, I'm not distracted by anyone's approach or movement. Often, I don't encounter any cars. By not wearing my glasses, I can see that someone has left their curtains open and the lights on, but I can't see enough detail to be distracted by what I see.

Within a quarter of a block, I voice this prayer: *Father, I'm here this evening to meet with you in silence. Please protect me from thoughts that are not from you. I'm trusting you. I feel vulnerable, but I desire deeply to walk with you, and if you have anything to say, let me know.*

The nights where silence is punctuated by God saying something fall under the category of solitude. Silence and solitude often dance together during the same evening, but they aren't the same discipline.

Many nights, I hear nothing. No profound thought. No insight. No clarity. No correction or conviction. No reminder. No observations. Many nights I return home only knowing as a matter of belief that I walked with my heavenly Father in the intimacy of silence that only close friends enjoy.

It is a profound idea, a remarkable concept, that God condescends from whatever occupies His attention to walk with me with no agenda or purpose beyond simply being with me as His friend. In fact, this theology is so profound that it requires the regular practice of spiritual silence to maintain the faith undergirding it.

To regularly create silence with the intent of meeting with God is to regularly practice the joy of being God's friend and He mine.

The neutrality of silence is your proactive determination at the outset to come to God with nothing more than your desire to be with Him. No agenda. No request. No prayer. No petition. Only the purity of your heart to say, *Father, I'm here in silence to spend time with you for the sake of who you are: my friend. Nothing more.*

The vulnerability of silence is the audacity of believing by faith that if you are silent, God will meet you in the intimacy of quietness. It is audacious to believe that you and God are so close, so intimate, so much of one heart, that you can be silent together. But it is a profound lack of faith to believe otherwise lest you cast doubt upon the thoroughness of Christ's reconciliation between you and God. Either you are close or you are not because you are either in Christ, drawn near to God, or you are not in Christ and are distant to God.

The presumption of silence—that you know God well enough, and that you are close enough as friends, to celebrate your friendship in silence—is so remarkable that the temptation to doubt God's closeness can be overwhelming. It's a theological conviction that requires consistent maintenance through devotion.

In practicing the discipline of silence, you deliberately challenge this temptation as false. By resolutely and frequently entering into silence, you seize upon your faith to implement into practice your belief that Christ truly did make all things right and that God has drawn you close.

Recall the summary statement in Hebrews 10:

> Therefore, brethren, since we have confidence to enter the holy place by the blood of Jesus, [20] by a new and living way which He inaugurated for us through the veil, that is, His flesh, [21] and since *we have* a great priest over the house of God, [22] let us draw near with a sincere heart in full assurance of faith, having our hearts sprinkled *clean* from an evil conscience and our bodies washed with pure water. [23] Let us hold fast the confession of our hope without wavering, for He who promised is faithful; [24] and let us consider how to stimulate one another to love and good deeds, [25] not forsaking our own assembling together, as is the habit of some, but encouraging *one another*; and all the more as you see the day drawing near.[194]

In silence you "draw near" in order to celebrate your closeness with God and His with you.

In the regular practice of silence, you do not "waver" under the assaulting temptation that friendship with God is too profound to be true.

In practicing the discipline of silence, and fostering the diligence in others, you "stimulate" the active, regular

---

[194] Hebrews 10:19-25.

practice of believing that in Christ Jesus the reconciliation between you and God is viable.

Close the door. Turn off the light. Leave your phone in the other room. When driving, turn off the radio and drive the speed limit to manage both literal and figurative noise. Take the back road versus the thoroughfare. If you have small kids, take turns superintending them so both you and your spouse have regular moments to practice silence.

In my article[195] "Quietness," I quoted Pascal: "The sole cause of man's unhappiness is that he does not know how to stay quietly in his room." Silence is powerful, silence is important, and silence takes us to a place both empowering and threatening.

The last thing in the world Satan wants you to believe is that you are close enough to God to be considered His friend and He yours.

If he can create doubt, then he diminishes your conviction that Christ's work is truly complete and that you are literally made right with God. Tolerate this frayed edge in the fabric of your theology, and even a gentle pull on the fraying edges by the duress in life and Satan's instigation— and the Book of Hebrews comes apart, i.e., there is a distance between you and God that Hebrews claims is not there given the completed work of Jesus. If Hebrews comes apart, then the Book of Romans comes apart. If Romans comes apart, then the Book of Galatians comes apart.

If it is possible for you to be distant from God, the doctrine of justification by faith found in Romans is in question. The legalism denounced as "another gospel" in Galatians has

---

[195] Gillham, Preston. "Quietness." *Lifetime.org.* Accessed, 18 December 2021. https://www.lifetime.org/articles/quietness

legitimacy for improving your standing with God. Salvation by faith alone in Christ as taught in Hebrews is insufficient to make you a child of God.

Sanctification, redemption, forgiveness, the inspiration of Scripture, the propitiation of Christ, the blood covenant between God and Jesus—none of these doctrines upon which your faith depends remain tightly woven together any longer. Your theology unravels like a cheap mat if the accusation is true that God is distant from you.

"The just, shall live, by faith," Paul writes in Romans and Galatians. Hebrews quotes the same passage originally found in the Book of Habakkuk.[196] The *just* and justification is the message of Romans. How you *shall live* is the message of Galatians. That you have life in Christ *by faith* is the message of Hebrews.

All your theological beliefs, and all the tenets by which you have hope in God through Christ, are anchored in the finished work of Jesus Christ and made yours by faith. Hebrews[197] states the only conclusion possible: Draw near to God and do so with confidence because of Christ's work. This is what Hebrews calls elsewhere the "anchor of the soul."[198]

The spiritual practice of silence is you placing yourself in position to celebrate with God, and He with you, the intimacy of a friendship so close that quietness is becoming and comfortable.

Your regular practice of the discipline of silence creates in you a sincere confidence that the friendship between you

---

[196] Romans 1:17; Galatians 3:11; Hebrews 10:38; Habakkuk 2:4.

[197] Cf.: Hebrews 7:18-25.

[198] Cf.: Hebrews 6:19.

and God is legitimate, true, and intimate enough to appreciate quietness.

And what if you create quiet, and practice the spiritual discipline of silence, and God says nothing? You wait, actively listening, trying your hardest to believe, to hear a word from God, to discern His voice. *Was that it? God? Did you say something? I'm listening—just so you know. Hello?*

But there is nothing. Not a sound from the Almighty. The quavering was only your indigestion.

While it is admirable to listen for God's voice—and God does speak—silence is no longer silence if someone is talking. In pressing to hear, you are demonstrating discomfort with silence.

You listen to God and converse with Him while practicing several of the other disciplines: Bible reading, confession, prayer, to name a few. But in silence, you are not doing. You are being, being present with God in your shared moment of silence. The power of this discipline is not what you hear, it is the silence itself and what that indicates about the nature of your relationship with God and God with you.

The practice of this discipline is to appreciate the intimacy of your relationship with God. Are you close enough, confident enough in your friendship with God, to be quiet in His presence?

But take note: This spiritual practice cuts both directions. You trust God in silence, but is God close enough to you, confident enough in you as His friend, to trust you with His silence?

You say, "Of course, of course. I'm in Christ and Christ is in me. I'm sealed with the Spirit, one with Him, and seated in the heavenly places. Just as you've pointed out, nothing can separate me from God or God from me."

And I say, "Perfect. The practice of the spiritual discipline of silence is designed to take the abstraction of the theology you just voiced and make it tangible, concrete, hard reality. If you are truly that close to God and He to you, then being in silence with Him will confirm for you that He and you are so tight as to be the best of friends."

In quietness, you will find your strength (Is. 30:15). Be quiet. Shh. Let your soul wait in silence for God (Ps. 62:1). If you hear nothing, celebrate that God trusts your friendship enough to trust you with His silence.

Questions and Considerations

1. Do you have silence in your life—meaning, in your soul? Are there *regular* times when your mind is quiet, your emotions calm, and your will not under duress? If so, where are these times, how are they created, and how resilient are they to life's noise? If not—there is not silence—what is necessary to create the discipline of silence in your daily life?

2. What do you believe this chapter is telling about why the practice of silence is important? In short, what does silence do for you that nothing else quite achieves or creates?

3. So, you practice the discipline of silence for the purposes conveyed in the chapter. But what if God practices silence with you? If you are saying nothing, and hearing nothing, now what?

TWELVE

The Spiritual Practice
of Solitude

> **"**
>
> *"Solitude is essential to reach the peak of any practice."*
>
> *Nitin Namdeo*

The alarm on his Wi-Fi device sounded at 5:00 AM. The room was pitch-dark. The night before he staged his clothing so he could dress by feel in the blackness.

Padding silently through the sleeping house, he carried his shoes to the bench beside the front door, sat down, slipped into his shoes, opened the front door, and closed it with a barely audible click as the latch caught.

He looked up and down the dim street. No one. Turning toward the copse of trees visible on the near-horizon, he began his trek, visualizing the path through the small wood, the sketchy trail across the meadow beyond, and the wilderness awaiting on the other side of the stream crossing.

As soon as he forded the stream, he took a deep breath, relishing the lonely place and its solitude, and began his prayers. Even in the dark, he knew this place more intimately than he knew the back of his hand.

"And in the early morning, while it was still dark, He [Jesus] arose and went out and departed to a lonely place, and was praying there," Mark writes of our Older Brother.[199]

I don't know how Jesus awakened while it was still dark. I'm quite certain it was not with a Wi-Fi device, but that He did so on a regular basis Scripture makes plain. Matthew, Mark, and Luke all note Jesus' propensity for slipping away into the wilderness, to pray alone, in a lonely place.

A place for my solitude in Arkansas

Nearly forty years ago, I read that my mentor, Mr. Drucker, went away for two weeks in August to reflect and

---

[199] Mark 1:35.

reconstitute his outlook. I was inspired and decided to follow his lead.

I didn't associate my decision with the spiritual practice of solitude, but as I retreated each Fall, the association did occur to me. As I have continued the practice, my concept and practice of this spiritual discipline has formed into one of the most treasured and beneficial disciplines in my life.

"Solitude liberates us from all the inane chatter that is so characteristic of modern life," Foster writes. "It liberates us from the ever-present demands that are put upon us; demands that in the moment feel so urgent and pressing but that in reality have no lasting significance. In solitude the useless trivialities of life begin to drop away. We are set free from the many "false selves" we have built up in order to cope with the expectations others place upon us—and we place upon ourselves. Solitude empowers us to walk away from all human pretense and manipulation."[200]

A place for my solitude in Colorado

---

[200] Foster, Richard J. "Understanding Solitude." *Renovare.org.* October 2014. https://renovare.org/articles/understanding-solitude

Like the other disciplines of the Christian life, solitude can be practiced in short bursts and impromptu venues. But for solitude to work its wonders, scheduled time of some duration is where the magic happens.

While I have moments of solitude that I create each week, I also set aside a day per month, and a week during the Fall for solitude and prayer. In the lines that follow, I'll describe my patterns and the underlying rationale. It's not important that you do what I do, like I do, but it is *essential* that you capitalize on my experience to form your own practice of the spiritual discipline of solitude.

Because the shift can be so subtle, let's review: You do not engage the spiritual disciplines to improve your status with your heavenly Father. Rather, you engage the spiritual disciplines because each practice is designed to help you comprehend, understand, and then appropriate into daily living essential aspects of what is true of God and true of you in relationship with God. As described by Foster, the disciplines place you on the spiritual path of grace and freedom in Christ. It is here that you encounter God and build the closeness indicative of friends and family.

Jesus said the most important thing in life is to love God.[201]

During His lifetime, Jesus demonstrated spiritual practices that advanced His comprehension, understanding, and consequential lifestyle as a man who knew God and walked with Him. It is one thing to declare theologically that you love God. It is altogether different to say that you *know* God closely and love Him. It is one thing to know *about* God, another to *know* God.

---

[201] Cf.: Matthew 22:37.

Hebrews says, "Remember those who led you, who spoke the word of God to you; and considering the result of their conduct, imitate their faith."[202] Christ modeled for you how to know God as Father and friend. And so it is that retreating to a lonely place in search of solitude facilitates your heart's desire to meet with your heavenly Father, discuss your life, and advance your awareness of who He is and who you are.

I've discovered that the inclination within me to pull away compliments God's desire to speak with me. Yes, there may be some experience of silence when I withdraw to the wilderness, but God respects my intentional devotion to create solitude, encourages me in my practice, and speaks because He knows I'm listening intently.

One day each month, I withdraw to a lonely place, create solitude, and spend the day listening to Father God's counsel, guidance, and perspective. For me, this typically means that I pull away to the state park about an hour from my house. It's large enough, remote enough, and I know the geography of it well enough that I can reliably create solitude.

Note that an aspect of this practice is that I *create* solitude.

I have go-to places that I've scoped out in advance as places that appeal to my soul and where I can control interruptions in order to create solitude. These are places that I define as wilderness: lonely places where I'm not distracted. Some are literally geographical wildernesses. These places are where I do my longer retreats. Other places are figurative wildernesses—like an airplane seat with noise-cancelling

---

[202] Hebrews 13:7.

earphones—or a less-traveled stretch of the Trinity River Trail near my home.

I have three or four wilderness places within an hour of home that I utilize monthly and three or four destinations to choose from annually for my retreats. By choosing my venues in advance, they are familiar places and I'm able to immerse myself into solitude right away without the distraction of getting acquainted with a new place.

I have discovered that the most beneficial time of solitude for me is my annual retreat in the Fall of the year. It took some time, and lots of trial and error, to figure out my routine. Like I said earlier, craft your own routine, but here's mine in hopes of flattening your learning curve.

The goal you hope to realize in practicing the discipline of solitude is an extended conversation with God about your life, your relationship with Him, and His vantage point regarding your life together. Your practice is to remove as many distractions as possible so you can listen with dedicated devotion. Place, pace, duration, and pattern are important components to consider as you practice spiritual solitude.

My customary pattern is to utilize my journals to remind me of my spiritual insights and issues over the year. I'll describe this process in a moment.

In the nearly forty years I've been taking a week for solitude, I've utilized a book to facilitate my thoughts on only four or five occasions. Obviously, it takes a special book for me to believe God wants us to spend our week of solitude sorting through a particular book's themes.

However, perhaps revisiting an important book you've read is just what you need to focus your solitude with God. While I've not devoted a week of solitude to it, I've spent a number of days and evenings either reading, reviewing, or contemplating David Gibson's book on Ecclesiastes. By my count, I've now been through his book nine times while utilizing various forms of solitude to my advantage.[203]

Perhaps it's a verse of poetry. After my first wife left—after I put her through college, and on our fifth anniversary, and her graduation day—taking most of our things with her and leaving me astounded and broken and professionally bankrupt, in solitude I contemplated: "Word I was in the house alone / Somehow must have gotten abroad, / Word I was in my life alone, / Word I had no one left but God."[204]

Maybe a passage of Scripture—not to study, per se, but to apprehend, to take aboard, and to let guide your life or your understanding of God. Speaking of whom, Jeremiah quoted God saying, "'But let him who boasts, boast of this, that he understands and knows Me, that I am the Lord who exercises lovingkindness, justice, and righteousness on earth; for I delight in these things,' declares the Lord."[205] God is saying that if you want to understand Him, understand what it means that He exercises lovingkindness, justice, and righteousness. This isn't a bad passage to consider in solitude: "Father, I would love it if you would talk with me about these three things in which you delight. Amen."

A key concept can guide your solitude. While it is not one of my finer periods of time, I will tell you that one evening

---

[203] Gibson, David. *Living Life Backward*. Crossway. Wheaton, IL. 2017.

[204] Frost, Robert. "Bereft." *The Poetry of Robert Frost*. Henry Holt and Company. New York, NY. 1969.

[205] Jeremiah 9:24 (23-24).

during my walk—my evening walks are times of created solitude—I heard God's voice in my head. Referencing the tenet of the faith, *sola Christos*, Christ alone, He asked in my thoughts, "So Pres, what will it be? Christ alone or Christ plus?" I knew with the "plus" God was asking me about the place my talents and abilities play in my standing with Him. I also knew the correct answer, the Christian answer. But rather than answer as I ought, I answered honestly and said, "Father, let me get back to you about that." I needed time to sort through motive and discern the place of capability. One evening, on my walk, I said, "Father, I'm ready to answer your question. With every ounce of my conviction and force of will, I declare without reservation, Christ alone!" It had been four years since God posed the question.

Solitude each evening served its purpose. In quietness, I listened, explored, examined. In time, I understood the confidence my heavenly Father had in my new self to sort through the motives underlying our relationship. In time, I understood the nature of my new heart. In time alone with Him, my heavenly Father coached me through my labor to trust—anyone, including Him. And one evening, in solitude, my wavering trust secured, I determined my conviction: "Christ alone!"

Yes, in this chapter I'm spelling-out my formula. No, my formula doesn't need to be yours, but you need a formula to create solitude that works for you and your Father in heaven. If you don't keep a journal, no worries. Dare to schedule solitude! Put it on your calendar, then ask, "Father God, I have scheduled time to be with you, to listen. What would you like to visit about?"

Typically, my longer periods of solitude capitalize on reviewing and expanding from my journals. The days I schedule to roam the state park rarely have an agenda. I simply create the solitude and figure if God has something on His mind, He'll let me know. I approach my evening walks similarly.

I didn't discuss God's question to me with Him every night for four years, and He didn't nag me about it either. But in various aspects of practicing the spiritual disciplines, I contemplated Father's question and my struggle to answer. Then, in the practice of solitude that looks like an evening walk, I was able to obtain with conviction my answer: "Christ alone!"

In all candor, had I not walked with God each evening, I wonder if I would have come to the conviction of *sola Christos!*

When I go away, I never take any discretionary reading material. No books, magazines, or Kindle for spare time. In the first place, I have no spare time. Second, I don't want anything to distract my solitude and focus. I never take my fly rod, or my bike, or my wife, or the dog, or a friend. All of these are distractions—noise—that risk disturbing my solitude.

Unless strongly convinced otherwise in advance, I pause my customary Bible reading for this time away. Yes, God speaks through Scripture when we practice the spiritual discipline of Bible reading and study, but this form of listening while reading Scripture is distinct from the listening done during solitude. Thus, unless led otherwise, routine Bible reading requires me to consider something other than the topics God has prepared ahead of my time away. Succinctly stated, Bible reading and study is about taking information aboard. The discipline of solitude is more about digesting information already on board.

So, I schedule my week away. I protect my schedule for two weeks before I depart as well as the weekend after I return home.

In the two weeks leading up to my departure, I review my journal entries for the year, i.e., since my last week of solitude. My journals are personal, electronic, and filled with all kinds of topics and musings that have importance and are just between God, the journal, and me. As I review, when I come upon an entry that is spiritual or that I deem relevant—a subjective but generous decision—I copy and paste the section into a fresh file.

Once I've gone through the entries for the year, copied and pasted as described into a new file, I will have created an edited file containing—broadly speaking—God's communications with me. The content of this file is the basis of my retreat. My presupposition is that God has been speaking to me all year, and if I will listen, He will elaborate upon His thoughts, and expand into other subjects during my solitude.

I have also exercised the discipline of solitude when I have a pressing matter on my mind that I need to discuss with God. I've also retreated into solitude after suffering a wound. But these practices of solitude are specialized retreats in that I pull away as necessary versus the planned withdrawal to lonely places already on my calendar.

In the days leading up to my departure, I visit with God about everything on my mind—all of my questions, concerns, dilemmas, issues, etc. It's a veritable mind dump—an emptying. Why?

Because when I depart for my week of solitude, I stop talking and devote myself entirely to listening.

At some point, I realized that I needed to define when my solitude begins, i.e., when I stop talking and start listening.

If I'm flying to my retreat, solitude begins the moment I step into the gate area for my flight.

I take this very seriously. Once I clear security, I go to the bathroom, then stand across the walkway from my gate and take final inventory of my thoughts. I scan through my mind for anything left unsaid to God as well as any phone call left undialed or loose end untied. Once satisfied, I step into the gate area and begin my week of solitude: no unrelated talking that is not essential, only listening.

I don't pray for my wife, you, my work, or my plans after I enter listening mode. For the next week, all I do is listen and respond to what God is saying in the wilderness of my lonely place.

If I'm driving, my solitude begins as soon as I turn out of my neighborhood. Similar to my routine at the airport, I pull to the curb before I leave my neighborhood, scan my thoughts for any unfinished business, and once satisfied, put the truck in gear and turn into listening mode and spiritual solitude.

Janelle Esker states, "Scriptural solitude is the biblical practice of temporarily withdrawing to privacy for spiritual purposes."[206] As a bit of an aside, Janelle is the mother of six who homeschools all. Before you excuse your failure to practice this discipline due to your demanding schedule, you might recalibrate your determination.

---

[206] Esker, Janelle. "The Spiritual Discipline of Solitude." *The PeacefulHaven.com*. June 27, 2018. https://www.thepeacefulhaven.com/the-spiritual-discipline-of-solitude/

The conviction within the discipline of solitude is that in quiet contemplation, you will hear from God in an extended conversation that is not possible during the regular ebb and flow of daily life. In creating a week—or an extended time—of quiet, you are practicing the skill of active listening. You are confronting the anxiety of loneliness with faith that in solitude you are not alone. Rather, you are alone with God. You are intentionally separating yourself from life's chaos to embrace time with no one else but Him. You are disciplining yourself with quietness to sophisticate your ability to hear God speak.

Thoreau said, "God is alone—but the devil, he is far from being alone; he sees a great deal of company; he is legion."

Before I depart, I make certain Dianne (my wife) feels secure, has what she needs, and concurs with the quietness and the solitary goal of my time away. I pledge to call each evening prior to dinner.

Once gone, my entry prayer into solitude is, *Father, I anticipate this week with you. I ask you to guard and guide my thoughts. Please speak to me about the things that concern us. To the best of my ability, I'm listening and desire nothing more than to hear from you, walk with you, and spend time with you.*[207]

Then, I begin a contemplative review of the computer file I created in advance. As I read, I consider myself engaging in prayer, one of the other spiritual disciplines that I will write about soon. As I read and thoughts come to me, based upon the prayer I prayed earlier (see italics), I believe in faith that I'm hearing from God. I make notes in my computer file, and as I write and additional thoughts come to me, I continue to

---

[207] Cf.: Matthew 6:6.

write, believing that as I do, I'm hearing from God and interacting with Him.

As an aside, God will never tell you anything that contradicts Scripture. Thus, the importance of knowing what's in your Bible and the theology it teaches. Reference again a sentence in my italicized prayer: *I ask you to guard and guide my thoughts.* It is my job to show up and listen. It is God's job to guard and guide. However, this doesn't mean you drop your spiritual guard. Meeting with your heavenly Father is the last place Satan wants you to be, so pay attention.

Once I'm on site, my pattern looks like this: Since it is likely afternoon when I arrive, and since I almost always retreat to the woods, I put on my boots and head out for a hike. I carry my phone, not to keep up with regular business, but as a recording device.

I typically switch my phone to airplane mode (no connection) until I choose to communicate. Dianne knows I will call before dinner. If she needs something right away, she knows to call the buddy I've enlisted to back me up while I'm away. In this way, I create solitude, and protect it, while easing my mind about the home front.

The phone is a dangerous distraction. I rarely take my week in a place with an internet connection, so my computer is not tempting. But the phone? Unless I'm off the grid—and one of my sites is—then as soon as I switch airplane mode off, the texts and voice mail notifications start dinging. Before I glance through the texts, I focus on why I am where I am and vow to not engage unless something is critical or POTUS has called. In truth, the President rarely calls and if there is a true crisis, someone else who is connected will take care of it. If Dianne or the buddy I've asked to back me up contacts me, I take the call. But in all my years, this has never happened.

I use my phone to record my thoughts—any thoughts of significance—while I'm hiking. I believe, by faith, that as I walk with a determination to listen, the thoughts I have are coming to me from God in honor of my intent to listen. Does not Scripture say to seek—and continually keep on seeking—the Kingdom of God and His righteousness and that everything concerning life's issues will be added to you?[208]

If my thoughts drift, I trust God will help me discern this and correct course. If I miss something God is saying, I trust Him to get my attention. If a thought comes to me that contradicts Scripture, I know that is not from God. As thoughts come to me that I know are not my own, I believe they are God's thoughts.

In all the years of practicing solitude, I've entered my week away during some very trying tumults. In retrospect, the advance preparation I've described has always put my mind in position to secure quietness when I step into the gate area or depart my neighborhood. My wife and friends have always had my back while I'm away.

After dinner is cleaned up, I return to my computer file. Often, in my scheduling for my week away, I coordinate my trip to coincide with a full moon. Thirty minutes before moonrise, I depart my quarters and hike the short-mile up the hill in the dark. No flashlight turned on so I arrive at the top of the hill with my eyes fully adjusted to the dark. Once in position, I stand quietly, listening, awaiting the moon's appearance.

---

[208] Cf.: Matthew 6:33.

As the moon emerges, the coyotes begin their yipping and howling at the lunar display. Since their curiosity has caused them to investigate me—meaning they've followed me as I walked up the hill—when they begin howling, I hear that they are close, all around me. I was counting on this when I scheduled my retreat with the full-phase of the moon.

For me, this is nothing short of divine—an appointment orchestrated by God, immersed in darkness, surrounded by His creatures. This is all part of how I go about creating solitude. The hike, the timing, the place—it's all part of the way in which I practice this spiritual discipline.

Once the coyotes have satisfied their curiosity with me and returned to their evening activities, I hike back down the hill in the dark—to avoid distraction while contemplating what just transpired—and return to my keyboard. When my thoughts are silent, I go to bed. Some nights I'm in bed by 9:00 PM. Sometimes, I don't lie down until the wee hours of the next morning.

I'm on God's time, not mine.

Solitude by lamp light, Colorado

I get up when I get up. I eat breakfast and return to my computer file. I listen at my keyboard until lunch. After lunch, I head out into the wilderness, recorder in my pocket.

My afternoons walking are not what Dad used to call "sweaty walks." Rather, I walk and I stop. I listen. I may sit by the creek. I do whatever I feel facilitates my ability to hear. I do whatever will engage all of my senses in my lonely place.

My pattern is to return home Friday afternoon. While I reconnect with Dianne, I have no other obligations for the weekend. I spend the weekend in review, cleaning up loose ends, taking long walks, and listening to Father's final words.

Once completed, I have an appended computer file of what God has said to me during my week of listening—my week of solitude—concerning all that we've discussed in the year prior and all that He has on His mind for the year upcoming. Invariably, God's thoughts throughout my week away are intimate, personal, close, and relational.

I do not use this time of solitude for study, preparation, or planning. Those are tended to elsewhere.

For my part, I've labored diligently to create solitude, put myself in place to listen, and captured what God has said to me. The only words I've spoken are requests for clarification, response to His thoughts, or engagement with what He is bringing to mind.

This routine works for me. A week is long enough for me to settle into the rhythm of solitude and get done what I need to do. On a handful of occasions, I've returned home with unfinished business. In these instances, I've cleared the next week of all I can to continue my listening.

I have friends who find three days is a good length of time. I used to coach my executive staff regarding solitude. When they were ready, I provided a three-day retreat in solitude for them as an executive perk.

I'm comfortable alone in the woods. Not everyone is and not everyone has access to literal wilderness. Dianne (my wife) goes away to a hotel—which requires its own set of parameters to manage distraction. What's important is that you pull away—that you create solitude and enter into it.

My routine is solid enough now that I can modify it to my advantage if I have a different amount of time or an irregular venue. This means my practice of the spiritual discipline of solitude is resilient and flexible.

It's advantageous that I'm my own boss. As I write to you, I understand that you may not have the flexibility that I have. But as Susan Cain notes, "We've known about the transcendent power of solitude for centuries; it's only recently that we've forgotten it."[209] My encouragement to you is to prioritize this practice and plan accordingly. Like I said initially, it is not important that you do what I do but that you do something to implement this discipline into your life.

What works for you?

Is there a question, an issue, a concern that won't resolve? That's a perfect agenda item for the practice of solitude.

---

[209] Cain, Susan. *Quiet: The Power of Introverts in a World That Can't Stop Talking*. Crown Publishers. New York, NY. 2013

Are you an extrovert? The practice of solitude is to your benefit in that it forces you to be quiet and draw your energy from time with God as opposed to drawing energy from being with people.

Are you an introvert? The practice of solitude is to your benefit in that it forces you to engage with God as opposed to isolating in self-sustainability.

As a Christian, you are in possession of a new heart that desires to know God and walk with Him. Listening to Him is the unique contribution the discipline of solitude makes to your heart's desire.

"And in the early morning, while it was still dark, He [Jesus] arose and went out and departed to a lonely place, and was praying there."

Questions and Considerations

1. How important is it that you have a week of solitude like I describe? What if two days is all you can create or manage? Is my week of solitude better than your two days? Are you sure based upon what you currently understand of the rationale underlying the spiritual practices?

2. What's more important: That you have a resource to guide your solitude or that you simply create solitude and embrace it? What does your answer tell you about the reason you engage in the practice of solitude?

3. How do you hear from God? What does His voice sound like? How will you know if He is speaking to you or whether its indigestion from the pizza you had last night? If you pray in preparation for solitude and tell God you are trusting Him to guide you, speak to you, and engage with you, how confident can you be that God will answer this prayer?

THIRTEEN

The Spiritual Practice
of Worship

"

"If I had my life to live over again, I'd have spent more

hours in worship."

Charles R. Swindoll

To write about worship feels like writing about the ocean. Vast. Deep. Immense.

Lehmann wrote: "Could we with ink the ocean fill, / and were the skies of parchment made; / were every stalk on earth a quill, / and everyone a scribe by trade; / to write the love of God above, / would drain the ocean dry; / nor could the scroll contain the whole, / though stretched from sky to sky."[210]

Worship should be remarkable and overwhelming. At its most basic, worship is reverent honor and homage due God. How exactly do you practice a spiritual discipline celebrating a subject who is omnipotent, omnipresent, omniscient...?

I suppose it is safe to say, there is no wrong way to worship God so long as God is the object of your effort to recognize and celebrate Him.

Moses took off his shoes. David danced—naked. He also sang and played an instrument. Job repented. Isaiah worshipped with obedience. Ezekiel laid on his face. Thomas renounced doubt. Mary uttered her *Magnificat*, Zacharias his *Benedictus*, and Simeon his *Nunc Dimittis*. The Centurion simply believed, and the woman with the hemorrhage?—well, she crawled through the throng of hangers-on to touch the hem of Jesus' garment.

Once upon a time, a young church on the island of Barbados asked if I would assist them in crafting a ministry strategy

---

[210] Lehman, Frederick M. "The Love of God." *Hymnary.org*. Accessed, 18 December 2021. https://hymnary.org/text/the_love_of_god_is_greater_far

for their island. My years working alongside these dear saints archive some of the grandest memories of my life.

The church gathered in an open-air pavilion each Sunday for worship and teaching. As they set up the chairs, they left the back of the pavilion open for dancing. It was the natural outpouring of the redeemed, people whose music and dance fill their culture as expressions of joy and celebration.

I dance if I must—or if alone while cooking dinner and listening to a waltz. Believe me, God would not be honored if I attempted to worship Him by dancing—and certainly not naked!

I remember hearing my friends' voices change as we entered puberty. Mine never did. I have a bass voice now and I had a bass voice in elementary school. My second-grade teacher gave me the "honor" of opening and closing the curtain during the musical program for our parents. I realize now I got to pull the curtain because she didn't want my low voice polluting an entire class of sopranos.

I worship with singing, but if anyone is around, I throttle my voice for fear I'll disrupt. But put me in the garage, or alone in my truck, and I joyfully sing to my Father in heaven. It's just an octave below normal.

I love music. When I was a kid our home was filled with music. By day, there was jazz. By night, Dad's radio picked up the wave-hop from WRR in Dallas, the classical station.

In the early 70s I had a job working at the First Presbyterian Church of San Clemente, California. On Monday nights, we drove to Costa Mesa for music night at Calvary Chapel. I didn't know it at the time, but what we know today as contemporary Christian music was being born.

I listen to contemporary Christian music, and sing along to my favorite songs. If I think about it, I can hear the melodies, but rarely recall the lyrics. This is interesting: If I *think* about the melodies. When I'm laboring to summon resolve, or to keep my wits about me in a tumult, or reassure my soul's disposition, the melodies that surface spontaneously are the grand hymns of the faith, complete with lyrics.

I'm not saying contemporary Christian music is inferior worship music. I am noting that music is moving, powerful, and the utilization of it is important for reassurance, determination, unification, and an offering of worship to God.

I've pondered if my inclination to the hymns versus the choruses is preference or importance: I say po-ta'-to, you say po-tah'-to; long hair, short hair; shirt tail in, shirt tail out; piano, guitar, organ, drum? As I've considered the question, there's more substance here than style I believe.

In his book, *Life Together*, Dietrich Bonhoeffer wrote, "Why do Christians sing when they are together? The reason is, quite simply, because in singing together it is possible for them to speak and pray the *same Word* at the same time."[211] The emphasis is mine, the capitalization his.

Bonhoeffer is asserting that unified singing of a biblical truth is a key component in building a life together as Christians.

This assumes of course that I know the song, that you know the song, that we all know the song. If I don't know the song, or don't recognize the tune, then I'm a spectator of your worship. Unless of course, you don't know the song either.

---

[211] Bonhoeffer, Dietrich. *Life Together*. Harper Collins Publishers. New York, NY. 1954.

Then we are both observers. At some point, if there are sufficient numbers in the room who don't know the chorus, then whatever inspiration is occurring is not corporate worship

Again, don't get me wrong. I'm not being critical of contemporary Christian music, but I am critiquing its efficacy in facilitating a group of individual's ability to reliably participate in corporate worship.

I'm not quite a musician. I play and read music, but I don't hear music well enough to naturally sing my part. Give me a piece of music with notes, not chords, and I can read and sing and participate.

By the time a worship chorus has been repeated, I've got the general melody. But it's still new, which means I'm concentrating on not making my joyful noise when those who know the song are resting from theirs. In other words, I'm concentrating to learn a song without making sour notes. I'm not worshipping.

It's a tricky business to teach individuals a song in the moment. To do so consistently and create corporate worship is more challenging yet, perhaps even improbable. If this model is the default, then the capacity of the church to worship corporately is impeded. Over time, the church's ability to enjoy the compounding benefits of corporate worship is compromised because the style constantly reboots the practice of corporate worship. The spiritual discipline that is intended to bring us collectively together in worship instead fractures individuals into solitary, isolated attendees.

Yes, there is benefit to listening to others worship. But only for so long. If you feel like an outsider each time you stand in the pew, it won't be long before corporate worship becomes pithy, irrelevant, and eventually a pointless expense of time.

Not to be ugly, but if you are destined to be an observer by design, why would you not stay home and listen to Brooklyn Tabernacle Choir, or the Gaither Band, or simply worship with your playlist?

Bluntly, if you can't sing with the church, and alongside your faith family declare lyrics in harmony that carry a strong message from the Word of God, then corporate worship is absent. What's labeled as corporate worship is a misnomer and practically irrelevant.

As I've repeated during these pages, the unified criticism of the church today by those leaving its rosters is that church is no longer relevant. This is a shame. A significant aspect of worship is corporate singing, yet we sabotage our collectivity by hamstringing the individual's ability to participate. Is it any wonder that the committed are fleeing the organized church like rats jumping from a burning ship?

But that's not all there is to worship because that's not all there is to God.

I sing. Oh do I ever sing. I lift my voice to God. I lift my hands to God. I sing in an octave that vibrates the windows, and I'm certain God hears my joyful noise—and He has yet to make me pull the curtain.

I also worship by listening. When I'm awake in the night, I sometimes step outside. Did you know that the Mockingbirds sing throughout the night? I go outside to listen. Their song helps me recognize my heavenly Father's creative ability—and I worship barefoot on the patio.

Scripture declares that Jesus Christ created everything in existence. I love a full moon. An aspect of my worship is stopping to stare, and say, "Nicely done, Brother. Nicely done."

Two weeks ago, I spent a week at an off-the-grid ranch in central Colorado. No electricity, no running water, only a spring about thirty yards from the cabin I rented.

I purposely drink more water than normal as bedtime approaches. This ensures that around 2:00 AM my bladder will awaken me. Before I go to bed, I lay out my shoes, my down coat, my stocking hat, my glasses, and my headlamp that has a flip-down red filter over the light. The red light doesn't ruin my night vision as I make my way out of the cabin. I stand in awe of the night sky. Not even when I rode my mountain bike through Arches National Park were there as many stars as I can see when I'm at the ranch—and celebrate, and recognize my Older Brother's creativity.

This summer, I followed a baby horned toad/lizard to see where he went. Watching him/her was a treat. Holding him a tickle. This inspired my worship of Father God.

Here in Texas, we have thunder and lightning storms that can be raucous, unruly, wild events. I stand on the porch, relishing the storm's transportation of my soul to worship Father and relish His power.

There is poetry that I read that gives voice to my admiration of God:

> I fled Him down the nights and down the days / I fled Him down the arches of the years / I fled Him down the labyrinthine ways / Of my own mind, and in the midst of tears / I hid from him, and under running laughter. / Up vistaed hopes I sped and shot precipitated / Adown titanic glooms of chasmed fears / From those strong feet that followed, followed after / But with unhurrying chase and unperturbed pace, / Deliberate speed, majestic instancy, / They beat, and a Voice beat, / More instant than the feet: / All things betray thee who betrayest me.[212]

Father God, thank you for pursuing, for never breaking, never failing, never flinching, never stopping, and never losing track of me. I recognize and worship you for this quality.

I'm a writer. An artist with words. Not only do I make every attempt to select the right word, the perfect word, but I am also conscious of how my words appear on the page. Glance through the pages of this book. The paragraphing varies to make each appealing to your eye. There are few words repeated in the same sentence—likely in the same

---

[212] Thompson, Francis. "The Hound of Heaven." *PoetryNook.com*. Accessed, 18 December 2021. https://www.poetrynook.com/poem/hound-heaven

paragraph. Scripture says to do my work heartily, as unto the Lord.[213] Thus, I consider my writing an act of worship.

Certainly, God is magnificent. His work phenomenal. His creativity is unmatched and His plans beyond ingenious. There is no question but that He is worthy of my worship. He has innumerable qualities named with glorious monikers conveying profound aspects of Him: omniscient, omnipotent, self-contained, immutable, sovereign, and the list goes on. I have no reservation declaring my worship.

I struggle to conceptualize the previous paragraph. I don't doubt it a whit, but the concepts are beyond large and imposing. God is great, distant; I am small and frail.

Certainly, He is high and lifted up and the train of His robe fills the temple, just as Isaiah declared. The angels gather around His throne, myriad upon myriad, and continually worship the King of kings and Lord of lords, God the Almighty.[214] Without reservation, I worship.

But the message of Christianity is also that God left heaven and came to me. He incarnated and took on human form. I celebrate—worship—His advent every December starting with the first Sunday after Thanksgiving. And taking on human form, He identified with my struggles, my sorrows, and my simple systems as a destitute soul.

In Jesus Christ, God is hungry, crying, sweating, tired; laughing, carrying on, kidding, and jousting; betrayed, misjudged, misunderstood, and ultimately, done inestimable wrong.

---

[213] Cf.: Colossians 3:23.
[214] Cf.: Isaiah 6:1; Revelation 5:11.

Me too.

And when I come to Him, I celebrate that He is close, that I am brought close, that He understands, and that I have every reason to worship with my trust. My simple, struggling trust.

Thank you, Father. Brother Jesus, thank you for coming, for living, for understanding. Spirit, I celebrate your presence within me. I honor you.

I run to you, as you invite. I gladly call you Father, Papa, Abba-Dad. I worship you for telling me this is how you would like to be approached and addressed.[215]

But when I go to the football game on Friday night and the announcer calls for a moment of silence "...to pray to the god of your choice," I worship magnificently. In my soul, I bow my knee under the Friday-night lights and say to God, *I declare you my Lord. I recognize you as King of kings; above you there is no other. I gratefully submit my life to you, yield my will to yours, and declare my unfettered allegiance to you, my Lord and my God. Amen*

After Paul penned, "Oh, the depth of the riches both of the wisdom and knowledge of God! How unsearchable are His judgments and unfathomable His ways!" he draws the simple conclusion, "I urge you therefore, brethren, by the mercies of God, to present your bodies a living and holy sacrifice, acceptable to God, which is your spiritual service of worship."[216]

---

[215] Cf.: Galatians 4:6.
[216] Romans 11:33-12:1.

Even the way you dress, carry yourself, and maintain your physical health is an act of worship.

Whatever advances your ability to honor, recognize, and celebrate God's divinity, character, love, mercy, and grace constitutes and qualifies as worship.

Contemporary choruses have their place in our worship. Obviously! But so do the hymns of the faith and the musical resources undergirding them to make corporate worship truly corporate.

Anything either hampering or facilitating the church's ability to unify and give robust expression of worship, together, as a collective of the divine family, is noteworthy and merits critical evaluation.

The corporate gathering of the church is in rapid decline.

My thesis in revisiting the disciplines of the faith is that we have drifted from our foundational fundamentals. Consequently, we are adrift from our moorings and suffering as a result.

The church as a bellwether for society is in grave question. Our outside reputation is that we are identified with a political party, not as the people of God. We are a voting bloc, not lights in the dark sea of humanity. Our spiritual leaders endorse political candidates as opposed to advancing the cause of Christ to address the existential questions of humanity.

The church is fundamentally failing itself, its members, and its place in society.

When something is fundamentally wrong, the diagnosis must be fundamental, and the solution must be a return to the disciplined practice of our fundamentals.

I didn't come up with these twelve spiritual disciplines. These are practices formed over two-thousand years of church history. They are rooted in Christ's life, not a book by Willard, or Foster, or Gillham. These disciplines are the best-practices our predecessors in the faith identified to help the individual as well as the church corporate maintain fidelity to the faith, to their hearts, to each other, and to God.

The logic is simple: If the church is not healthy, then it only makes sense that we must return to the practice of our fundamentals. If society's critical concern is existential—acceptance, worth, significance, importance—then society's critical concern is not political, financial, or governmental. Society's crisis is spiritual. If this logic holds, then this must become the church's finest hour.

The criticism of the church is that it is no longer relevant to daily life. Of course, the Gospel has not become irrelevant, so what the criticism is telling us is that the practice of the church has lost its ability to facilitate the Gospel in daily practice and within civil society.

Of the twelve disciplines, the spiritual discipline of worship is the foremost practice of how the church functions corporately. That this corporate act of worship is impeded, even compromised, by style should capture our attention.

If it is not possible for us to sing together, then it is unlikely we will suffer together.

I'm not advocating for an either/or choice in corporate worship. Perhaps a blend is feasible. If you are a leader of worship, experiment. But keep in mind: What fails to unify us, divides us.

The practice of the spiritual discipline of worship is an historic discipline because it advances both individually and corporately our joy, celebration, and affirmation of who God is, who He has declared us to be, and what His Word is to us. Worship unifies us as we declare together, at the same time, the wonder and glory of God and His Word.

Richard Foster says, "Without joyous celebration to infuse the other disciplines, we will sooner or later abandon them. Joy produces energy. Joy makes us strong."

Questions and Considerations

1. The spiritual practice of worship is important, but how defined is your worship? What does your worship look like? How many forms of worship are you aware of in your practice of this discipline? Whatever your answer, is this okay, especially if you practice a form of worship that is outside what is considered the norm? What is your rhythm of worship: momentary, daily, weekly? Whatever your answer, does this rise to the level of a discipline of worship in your life?

2. This chapter makes a direct correlation between what you do for a living and your spiritual practice of worship. What do you think? If you are a student studying literature, is what you do as spiritually worshipful as your pastor studying Scripture for Sunday's sermon? Is there profane work and divine work? Is teaching a Bible study more spiritual than accounting? In short, how do you enter into worship and practice its discipline as a routine of your life?

3. Of all the spiritual disciplines examined in these pages, the practice of worship is the most corporate, meaning: it is a discipline that often occurs alongside others. Must worship include corporate worship to fully practice the discipline of worship? Why or why not and how do you adjust your practice of worship if you are not satisfied with your current practice of this discipline? Can you worship alone? How important is corporate worship?

FOURTEEN

The Spiritual Practice
of Prayer

"

"To be Christian without prayer is no more possible than

to be alive without breathing."

Martin Luther

A friend told me that he appreciated a series of articles I wrote on the spiritual disciplines, which was nice to hear. He went on to say, "But I don't like the word discipline."

Perhaps no other aspect of Christianity has been subjected to more legalistic application than have the spiritual disciplines. This means a careful examination of the practices is suspect from the beginning.

A nationally acclaimed minister told me, "Look, 'spiritual discipline' is not a biblical term. You're teaching heresy."

I replied, "You're correct. The word 'spiritual' and the word 'discipline' do not appear side-by-side in Scripture. But your literalness avoids, excuses, perhaps denies, the force of Scripture to guide our lives. Paul said to Timothy, 'Discipline yourself for the purpose of godliness.'[217] Perhaps we should rename these practices the 'godly disciplines.'"

You are free from the religious instruction teaching that *you must* in order *for God to*. You are free from trying to get close to God. You are one with Him. There's no way to get closer than that. But these declarations pertain to legalism not godly practice.

Granted, you can take almost any Scripture and turn it into a legalistic requirement, including the spiritual disciplines. Doing this doesn't make the principle or practice wrong. It identifies a misguided motive. Just because a biblical principle can be mis-applied does not mean it is flawed. Rather, the Scriptural truth is abused by the one teaching the error.

Renunciation of the spiritual disciplines for fear of legalistic application is irresponsible—a deflection of personal responsibility to engage the rigor of spiritual discipline while dispelling any legitimacy for a legalistic usage. Not only did the teacher I reference demonstrate simplistic exegesis, he revealed a rudimentary avoidance of how faith must include behavior and grace must include practice.

Scripture declares that as a new person in Christ you are created to perform good works.[218] Transformed by the redemptive work of Jesus Christ, you are designed to function—to perform—according to God's original intention.

It is true that you are free from a performance-based acceptance with God. It is also true that you are expected to

---

[217] 1 Timothy 4:7.
[218] Cf.: Ephesians 2:10.

perform in keeping with your freedom and according to your spiritual design.[219] This freedom-by-design requires discipline to bring freedom into daily life.

Recall again the opening quotation from Aristotle: "Through discipline comes freedom." Ann Voskamp puts it this way: "Daily disciplines are doors to full freedom."

Still, the Bible is candid about discipline: "All discipline for the moment seems not to be joyful, but sorrowful." Paul reports buffeting his body, training like a boxer, winning, and running with endurance.[220]

When it comes to discipline, the question is not should you discipline yourself, but how and why.

The answer is simple yet profound.

You discipline yourself as Christ disciplined Himself because doing so enables you to realize—to recognize, perform, and enjoy—your heart's true desire. And what does your new, redeemed heart[221] desire? More than

---

[219] The New Testament is filled with imperative statements. My rough estimate is that there are over 1500 of these imperatives, i.e., instruction the author intends for you to act upon. There are approximately 75 occurrences of words conveying practice, discipline, formation of skill, achievement, determined performance, development of sound thought, exercise of restraint, reigning in of passions to avoid temptation, etc. My Greek concordance contains about seven pages of references for the words translated "perform" and "exercise." Clearly, faith and behavior, grace and practice, mercy and individual response go hand-in-hand. Yes, these biblical principles can be mis-applied, even abused, but that must not be an excuse to dismiss, avoid, denounce, or renounce their appropriate usage and determined practice. It is essential to your wellbeing, and our corporate health and effectiveness as the church, to diligently figure out the correct, applied practice of the spiritual disciplines based upon the full counsel of the Bible. Anything short of this diligence is what Bonhoeffer deemed "cheap grace," and by his estimation and history's record, cheap grace will result in a church that is irrelevant.

[220] Cf.: Hebrews 12:11; 1 Corinthians 9:24-27; Hebrews 12:1.

[221] Cf.: Ezekiel 36:26.

anything, you desire to genuinely know—not know *about*, but sincerely *know*—and understand your heavenly Father, God.

As I have written previously, Richard Foster gives the word picture of the Christian life being like a mountain path. On one side of the path is a precipitous drop into the depths of legalism, i.e., performance-based acceptance with God. On the other side is the dark valley of license, i.e., taking impudent advantage of God's grace in justification to follow after sin's enticements. But on the path, which Foster identifies as the spiritual disciplines, is where your heart longs to be because it is on this path that you encounter God. Walking with God, you grow to know God, to understand how He thinks, operates, loves, and persists in lovingkindness.

The spiritual disciplines, the spiritual practices of the faith, are the path that place you in position to realize your heart's desire.

From this vantage point, the disciplines are not onerous burdens of religious requirement. They are the means to a desired end.
The spiritual practices set you free to fly with God. In the imagery of Plato, the spiritual disciplines return to your soul the wings that were lost to you as a descendant of Adam. In the poetry of David, the disciplines are where God gives him feet like a ram enabling him to scale mountain heights his enemies can't climb. Habakkuk used the same imagery to console his soul with the impending invasion of the Chaldeans.[222]

---

[222] Cf.: Psalm 18:33; Habakkuk 3:19.

Like the other spiritual practices, prayer is neither obligation nor regulation. Rather, prayer is the active, conversational engagement of your heart and soul with the heart and soul of God.

Prayer as a discipline is nothing more than a regular, habitual pattern of conversation with God—a relational default that is so routine for you that it is your normal disposition as you approach each day's demands. When Scripture says, "Pray without ceasing,"[223] this practice is the application.

How then should you pray?

Some prayers are formal, others casual. Some are thoughtful. Some intimate, caring, and tender. Some are serious and some hilarious. Some are voiced, some are thought. Some have words and others do not.

Your relationship with God completely encompasses all that you are, all that is in your heart to say, and all that your soul can conceive.

My buddy Ralph Harris[224] writes about, "Loud prayer. Angry prayer. Sloppy prayer." He says, "I've learned I'm safe to express the terribles and awfuls and dreadfuls to God, who proves He is the antidote in me for the poison I'm experiencing."

When Jesus' disciples said, "Lord, teach us to pray," He obliged them with a form, an outline: "When you pray, say, 'Father, hallowed be Your name. / Your kingdom come....'"

---

[223] 1 Thessalonians 5:17.

[224] See: RalphHarris.org.

The church recognizes this as the model prayer in that it encompasses all aspects of our communication with God.[225]

The opening line of prayer in the *Gloria Patri* of the liturgy reads, "Glory to the Father, and to the Son, and to the Holy Spirit: as it was in the beginning, is now, and will be for ever. Amen."[226]

As Peter is drowning, he prays, "Lord, save me!" The outcast woman prays, "Lord, help me!" Offended and indignant, Martha prays, "Lord, do you not care?"

How do you pray?

John Piper writes, "Pray to the Father in the name of Jesus by the power of the Holy Spirit. This is the general form of prayer in Scripture. But, from time to time, 'Maranatha! Lord Jesus come!' is not a bad prayer."

The point is not how you approach God in prayer but that you come to Him.

God is no more impressed or moved with, "Almighty God, maker of heaven and earth," than He is put off with a wrenching, "Oh, God! Please help me."

Ralph writes again, "My prayers with God are conversational, not formal. And in that, there is room for calm, gentle, quiet and listening, as well as for volume adjustments, hand waving, fiery feelings, bad grammar, and bad vocabulary. That's all there because that's all me with

---

[225] Cf.: Luke 11:1-4.

[226] Guilbert, Charles Mortimer, Custodian. *The Book of Common Prayer*. Oxford University Press. New York, NY. Certified, February 1990.

God. He knows me at every moment already, so I don't change myself to create a better moment."

The Bible states that Christ is in God, you are in Christ, and Christ is in you.[227] For this position to be altered or tarnished would require that God change His mind, which He set before laying the foundations of the world, or that the finished work of Jesus Christ become unfinished.

Therefore, you can speak and pray, you can think and pray, you can pre-dispose yourself for an event and pray. In fact, you can utter unintelligible sounds and Scripture says the Spirit prays for you in your groanings.[228]

Brennan Manning says, "A little child cannot do a bad coloring; nor can a child of God do bad prayer."

God says, "Come." He tells you to pour out your heart to Him. He literally instructs you to "fling your concerns in His general direction," so there's no need to even organize your prayer. The humility of God is that He stoops to where you are rather than requiring you to rise where He is.[229]

Willink and Babin teach that a good leader is not put off by questions. In fact, good leaders expect and invite questions and conversation.[230]

If this is true of earthly leaders, then it is certainly true of God. He invites your questions, even your disagreement. He challenged Job to debate Him and Isaiah to argue with Him.

---

[227] Cf.: John 14:20.

[228] Cf.: Romans 8:26.

[229] Cf.: Matthew 11:28-30; Psalm 55:22..

[230] Willink, Jocko and Babin, Leif. *Extreme Ownership*. St. Martin's Press. New York, NY. 2015, 2017.

Yes, God is God, King of kings, and Lord of lords. But He also is your Father. Scripture says the Spirit guides you to call Him, Abba/Daddy.[231]

Do you recall the photographs of John Jr. with his dad, President John F. Kennedy? The pictures provide an earthly inkling of your heavenly relationship with God. Just as a child is not obligated by formality with their father, neither is a child of God constrained with their heavenly Father.

Ask. Seek. The force of the grammar is to keeping asking and keep seeking. Continuously. To the extent you can

---

[231] Cf.: Romans 8:15.

understand, God wants you to know and understand Him and His ways.

Let's face it though: God knows everything. So, what's the point of prayer?

Obviously, you don't pray in order to inform God or update Him on your life. Thus, from God's vantage point, the only possible reason for you to pray is that he loves interacting with you.[232] All you have that God desires is you. So, come. Pray.

Do you ever call your spouse just to hear their voice? Do you ever pray just to hear God's voice, and Him yours?

Willink and Babin go on to say that while great leaders entertain questions and even debate, sometimes a question can't be answered and a plan won't be changed.[233]

There are biblical instances of prayer where persistence results in the prayer's desired outcome. But the majority of prayers asking for a particular outcome are not answered according to the prayer's wishes.

The Bible reports that Daniel prayed for protection when cast into the lion's den. God responded and shut the mouths of the lions. But history records that countless Believers were fed to the lions and died torturous deaths. Is there any doubt these folks prayed with faith, believing God for protection, even while their bodies were being torn asunder?[234]

---

[232] Packer, J.I. *Praying the Lord's Prayer*. Crossway Publishers. Minneapolis, MN. 2007.

[233] Willink and Babin. Ibid.

[234] Cf.: Daniel 6:16-24; Hebrews 11:35b-40. We love to hear stories of deliverance like Daniel's, but shy from stories like the "others" mentioned in Hebrews 11:35b. For every story of deliverance from the lions, there must be thousands of stories about God's grace

Prayer is not a potion. Prayer is not magic. Prayer is not a posture. God doesn't hear a kneeling prayer better than He hears a desperate prayer or a grateful prayer at mealtime.

Prayer is a relational exchange between you and God. Since you and God are never separated, there is no such thing as unanswered prayer. God would not tell you to come to Him only to turn away, ignore, and disavow you.

My encouragement is to be careful how you define answered prayer. Sometimes God's answer is a torrent, at times a nod or a wink, and often the intimacy of silence is plenty of reply in His estimation.

While God always answers, God does not always answer as you hope, wish, or plead for in this life. God responds to every prayer, but on His terms and with His foreknowledge. Your confidence can be—must be—that God who is absolutely good can do nothing shy of His absolute best for both you and Him. But for this trust to superintend your daily outlook, you must also realize that God works from and for eternal purposes. At times you are privileged to see God's hand in real time and at times you are entrusted to believe the goodness of His heart toward you and the eternity you and He have together.

The Apostle Paul was detained under house arrest from AD 60-62.[235] Putting myself in Paul's shoes, I would struggle to understand why God would leave me in prison when my sincere desire was to travel and preach the Gospel. But while imprisoned, Paul wrote four of the thirteen books he penned that are contained in the New Testament:

---

during martyrdom by lions. If prayer is only good for sporadic deliverance and not for grace in times of suffering, then prayer is limited and God either distant and/or capricious.

[235] Ephesians 6:18-20.

THE SPIRITUAL PRACTICE OF PRAYER

Ephesians, Philippians, Colossians, and Philemon. One has to wonder if Type-A Paul would have written if God had not left him chained to his guard.

Paul prayed diligently that God would let him travel to Rome to preach.[236] Instead, he was detained in Corinth. So, disappointed with God's denial, Paul instead wrote a letter to the church in Rome. It is the greatest treatise of systematic theology contained in Scripture, but it opens with a clear statement by Paul of how frustrated he is to be writing as opposed to traveling to Rome.[237] God declined Paul's request to preach in Rome knowing in His foreknowledge that in two millenia you needed access to the Book of Romans. Paul was disappointed with God's denial. You thank God for denying Paul's request.

Ask, in faith, trusting, but understand that God's answer may be beyond your pay grade.

Recall that Jesus, the perfect man, prayed in the Garden of Gethsemane. His human prayer was so fervent, so anguished, that He sweat anxious drops of blood.

Note that Jesus prayed the same prayer, "Father, deliver me," multiple times. Even Jesus' persistence in prayer did not render the desired outcome. Realizing what was coming, He prayed passionately for an alternative plan—and was crucified anyway.

So, telling God repetitively, and with energy, what's on your mind is fine.

---

[236] Cf.: Romans 1:8-15.
[237] Cf.: Romans 1:11-13.

However, God knows the ultimate plan and you do not.

Therefore, it is imperative in your praying to trust the wisdom and goodness of God lest you believe yourself slighted and abused by an indifferent deity. God is good, and He must be good all the time or He is not good at all. However, just because He is good doesn't dictate that His answer will be to your liking.

Have you considered what would have transpired if God answered Jesus' prayer in Gethsemane as He requested?

For all of His sweating and anguished prayers for deliverance, Jesus also declared His trust in God's foreknowledge: "Father, if you are willing, remove this cup [of suffering and death] from me; yet not my will, but yours be done."[238]

In practicing prayer, especially when you are anxious or sense an impending trauma, it is healthy for your soul to follow your Older Brother's practice in prayer and say, "Father, I've expressed my opinion and I thank you for hearing my prayer. However this works out, I trust you and your good will toward me."

Like the Preacher taught in Ecclesiastes,[239] James also notes the futility of arrogantly making plans as if your life is yours to foreknow and manage. He counsels you to pray this way: "If the Lord wills, we will live and also do this or that."[240]

The commanding, insisting, believing, declaring prayer of positive confession taught by some teachers is problematic, their sincerity notwithstanding. The disrespect of

---

[238] Luke 22:42.
[239] Cf.: Ecclesiastes 1:2.
[240] James 4:13-17.

demanding that God do what you declare; the arrogance of believing you know enough, are insightful enough, or are sufficiently prescient to command God's conduct causes me to wince.

Psalms recalls that Israel became demanding of God when they were in the wilderness. They tempted Him, no doubt taunting Him to answer their demands. So, God answered their demand... but sent a wasting disease among them.[241]

God invites you to freely come to Him with any concern and approach, like a child does their parent. But any healthy relationship hinges on mutual respect.

James instructs you to pray with faith. Asking. Believing. Not doubting. Failing to pray with confident belief results in a tumultuous lack of resolve, like waves lapping the seashore, James writes. In fact, a doubting prayer is an ineffective prayer. God wants you to confidently come to Him with transparent honesty. You are His child. Christ is your Brother. The Spirit is your Helper. Doubting this renders you doubleminded and unstable because it is an affront to God's redemption of you.[242]

How you approach God in prayer is indicative of what you believe about God and about yourself. Clearly, God knows more than you. Yet, you contend against the giants of life in this fallen and dark world. Discussing your view with God, and He His view with you, means your prayer together might seem incongruent. The common denominator between you and God that establishes your mutual respect

---

[241] Cf.: Psalm 106:14-15.
[242] Cf.: James 1:5-8.

as inviolable is His goodness. Herein is your confidence to trust Him.

As you read in the chapter on the practice of fasting, in March of 1982 I began a daily, 24-7 odyssey with physical pain. Over the years, I've seen every type of practitioner you can name and a lot you've never heard of. I've been exorcised, dieted, exercised, anointed, stretched, stuck, struck, burned inside and out, popped, pressurized, frozen, cauterized, immobilized, anesthetized, categorized, demonized, renounced as a remorseless sinner, and been more demoralized at times than you want to know about.

I've sweat through my clothes resisting pain on more occasions than I can number. I've cursed, and cried, and cajoled. I've stood by the airplane bathroom, smelling that smell, over thousands of miles, to more destinations than I can count because it hurt too badly to sit down. Countless nights, not even the dog was faithful enough to sleep with me because of my tossing and turning.

I've prayed every prayer, read all the right books, and felt the hands of those gifted with biblical miracles of healing and prophecy pleading with God for my healing and deliverance. Nothing.

I've declared in faith, walked in faith, believed in faith, professed in faith, and to date am denied relief though still believing. I've tried thanking God, rejoicing in all things, yielding my rights, and wielding the sword of the Spirit against the dark adversaries in unseen places who torment my physical frame. Nothing.

For me, sincerely praying, "Father, not my will but yours be done," has been a torturous disposition to acquire and at times remains a tenuous hold.

But now, more often than not, after years of practicing prayer, I can locate this sincere footing within my soul. Over time, my difficulty has become a high place, like the high place David and Habakkuk spoke of, where my feet are like hind's feet and I find solitude in the places Father frequents.

Foster is correct. My practice of prayer has resulted in conversations, convictions, and character with Father God and about Him that I never would have had if He had answered my prayers for healing in 1982.

The spiritual practice of prayer, like the other disciplines, isn't intended to achieve an earthly end, but to position you to realize your heart's ambition: to know God and understand His ways.

One day, like my brothers Mason and Wade,[243] I too shall be released from this life and enter heaven's gates. Pain will be left behind.

I have little notion of what heaven will be like, although I'm sure it will be fine. But at some point, once inside the pearly gate, my anticipation is Father saying to my Older Brother and me, "Come on. Let's go discuss life. Spirit, make certain my younger son understands, please." And the waltz of prayer will begin, four friends conversing with no fallen impediment between them.

My hope is that through the spiritual practice of prayer here, my conversation there is a natural, easy transition. You know, like picking up where we left off, but without an, Amen.

---

[243] Cf.: Gillham, Preston. "Wade." *PrestonGillham.com*. January 27, 2017. https://www.prestongillham.com/blog/wade

Questions and Considerations

1. The more Reformed in their theological persuasion explain human failure, and Christian sinning, as caused by a dark and wicked heart. Their biblical justification for this comes from the Old Testament prophets like Jeremiah and Ezekiel. However, you can make a theological case using the same prophets (cf. Jeremiah 31:31-33; Ezekiel 36:26-27) that the Believer is possessed of a new heart that desires what God desires and desires to know God personally. *Rigorous Grace* takes this latter approach and explains human failure and a Christian's poor performance on the basis of Romans 7, et al. A Reformed theologian has a difficult time explaining why a Christian has a desire to know God if their heart is desperately wicked. But as *Rigorous Grace* puts forward, a Believer endowed with a new heart is by default filled with a desire to know God because it's in his heart to do so. So, look into your heart. What do you desire? Do you desire to please God or be rebellious toward God? I'm not asking what you do or feel, rather I'm asking what you desire. Why is this important to discern? If you are inherently still rebellious toward God, then the last thing you want to do is interact with God in transparent, honest, heartfelt prayer. So, what do you desire?

2. Scripture states that God is love. Therefore, God is obligated to love you by His own essence, i.e., God loves

you because He must. Here's the question: Yes, God loves you, but do you believe God likes you? If you walked into a room where God was, when He turned and saw you, what would His expression be? How does this view of God inform your practice of prayer, i.e., discussion with God?

3. As you consider the discipline of prayer and your practice of it, what do you think your conversation with God will be like when you arrive in heaven? Will your practice of prayer be better, more meaningful, more heartfelt, more sincere... more something—or will you simply take up the conversation you and God were having just before you departed this life to enter into heaven? How does your answer inform and guide your practice of prayer today?

FIFTEEN

The Spiritual Practice of Soul Friendship

> **"**
>
> *"There is nothing on earth more to be prized than true*
>
> *friendship."*
>
> *Thomas Aquinas*

The underlying rationale for the spiritual disciplines is to model our spiritual practices after those demonstrated by Jesus Christ. I recently presented this rationale to a group of church and ministry leaders. Among other pushbacks, several declared I was advocating that WWJD was an appropriate course of action.

WWJD? That's right: Asking, "**W**hat **w**ould **J**esus **d**o?" and then attempting to replicate Him.

It was a thinly veiled accusation of legalism, an assertion that I was advocating for living the Christian life via the power of self-resolve—the power of the flesh. They accused that by emulating Jesus, I was teaching that you sanctify yourself before God.

It's a bogus accusation, but worthy of a few words of explanation: WWJD is an inspirational, provoking question, but it is conceived upon two fallacies. First, WWJD assumes that you can do what Jesus would do. Second, WWJD assumes Jesus is not present.

Let's be clear: God has not called you to live the Christ-life, the Christian life. That's an impossibility. It's backward theology. God has called you to let the indwelling Christ live His life through you.

It is bad theology to say that you get better—more holy, more sanctified—as you try harder to live a godly life. This may be the theology of all other religions in the world, but this is not the orthodox, pure, systematic theology of Christianity.

Practicing the spiritual disciplines does not progressively sanctify you—make you holier and holier until God says, "Okay, child. That'll do." You are either totally sanctified or you are totally unsanctified. You are either holy or you are unholy. Because God is absolutely holy, His standard for holiness is absolute.

Your acceptance with God—your holiness as far as He's concerned—is determined singularly by what you've done with Jesus Christ's offer of redemption. If you have surrendered your life to Him, then you are alive in Christ, justified, sanctified, declared holy. If you have rejected His offer of redemption, then you are excluded from the life of Christ and are dead to God.

Acceptance with God is binary: You are either in Christ and accepted or you are not in Christ.

Practicing the spiritual disciplines has nothing to do with sanctification, holiness, justification, righteousness, or acceptance with God. All of these tenets of the faith are determined and satisfied in and through Jesus Christ. You are the beneficiary of these tenets of the faith when you become a Believer.

This is the Gospel of Jesus Christ. Redemption is remarkable. This is why we call the Gospel *amazing* grace.

It only makes sense that you examine the life of your Older Brother to conceptualize the inconceivable, believe the unbelievable, and grasp that His life can and will empower your life now.

As such, it is not only possible, but it is *the divine intent* that you know, understand, and actively embrace God as your Father, just as Jesus demonstrated.

Early in His ministry, Jesus selected twelve followers, the folks we know as His disciples. Yes, He trained them, prepared them, blessed them, and sent them out as sheep among wolves. They carried the Gospel into the world after their empowerment with the Spirit. All but John died martyrs and he died an exile on the island of Patmos.

At first blush, Jesus selected twelve to ensure His Gospel legacy had longevity. But even though Christianity thrives in the hearts of millions, it is a stretch of rationale to attribute the spread of Christianity to the fidelity of the disciples. Yes, they dedicated their lives to the cause of Christ and died faithful, but they were hardly exemplary.

Brennan Manning remarked that Jesus referred to Peter as "the Rock," but in reality he was a pile of sand. You can make similar cases for the others. The survival and progress of

Christianity is multi-faceted and is the voluminous study of the church—which I will spare you in these few pages!

The point for us is, there has to be something besides legacy going on in Jesus' mind when He selects the twelve. We grasp what the disciples did, and we are the beneficiaries of Christianity, but what did Jesus Himself hope to gain by surrounding Himself with the twelve?

Jesus, God-incarnate, launched a divine initiative that we know as the Gospel of Christianity. But Jesus, the fully-human man, laid aside His divinity and took upon Himself flesh and blood. He loved, and hurt, and ate and drank, and laughed, and grieved—so that after all was said and done, Jesus could say, "I suffered in every way you suffer. I lived so completely that I identify with all aspects of what it means to be human. I understand."[244]

In His human understanding, Jesus knew He required friends. Not just friends with whom He fished, but friends who knew His soul, friends with whom He bonded. This soul friendship that Jesus demonstrated is the essence of the spiritual discipline of practicing soul friendship.

Milton observed that "no sparrow lacks a friend with whom to roam." The one whose eye is on the sparrow, who notes when each little avian body falls,[245] understood that He too needed—required—friends with whom to roam. So, He selected for Himself twelve in hopes they would become soul-level friends.

Andrew and Peter, brothers, fishermen. Both martyrs by crucifixion, but Peter, considering himself unworthy to die

---

[244] Cf.: Hebrews 2:9-18.
[245] Cf.: Matthew 10:29-31.

like his friend Jesus died, requested to be hanged upside down. Tradition holds that Andrew was tied to an X-shaped cross, thus prolonging his death by days. The word is he preached about his friend Jesus from his cross until succumbing to death.

Bartholomew, a man with royal blood. Jesus chose this man, also known as Nathaniel, because he had no guile—there was nothing false or contrived about him. He was honest and without pretense. He succumbed to death while being fileted like a fish because he would not renounce his friend, Jesus.

James and his brother John, both fishermen, both intolerant, aggressive, and ambitious. James lost his head to Herod, the first of Jesus' friends to be martyred for his loyalty. Attempts were made on John's life, but the one known for his deep love, died in exile for his loyalty to the one whom he loved: Jesus.

James son of Alpheus, an exemplary and fiery man, known for his strong character, died while his body was being sawn apart. The reason for his death was his refusal to renounce his faith in his friend, Jesus.

Thaddaeus, also a son of Alpheus, gifted with miracle powers. Like his brother, Thaddaeus was martyred for his friend while in Ararat. His execution was conducted with arrows.

Judas, the friend who failed. He betrayed his friend with a kiss in exchange for a few coins totaling less than the amount prescribed by law to pay for a slave accidentally killed. Grieving his betrayal of his friend, Judas committed suicide by hanging.

Matthew, a usurious tax-collector and a hated man. Before his martyrdom, he wrote a biography of his friend in both Greek and Hebrew. Foxe reports that Matthew was staked to the ground with halberds, a two-handed axe-spear, and beheaded for his belief in and teaching about his friend, Jesus.

Philip, the first to leave everything and follow Jesus. He was possessed of a warm and generous heart that out-paced his mind's ability to trust. In the end, while in the process of being hanged for belief in his friend, requested that his body be wrapped in papyrus rather than in linen, not wishing to be interred by the same process as his friend Jesus was at His death.

Simon, a member of the Zealots. Fanatical, loyal, dedicated to the Jewish resistance against Roman rule, pure-hearted, pledged to faithfulness and suffering without remorse. In time, he was the friend who championed following Jesus willfully, versus the compulsion required by the Zealots. Justus Lipsius reports that Simon was sawn in half for his friend.

Thomas: pessimistic, cautious, calculating, but once his mind was decided, courageously loyal. He was executed by spear while in India. His crime was failure to renounce Jesus, in whom he believed.[246]

---

[246] Cf.: Editors. "How Did the Twelve Apostles Die?—Where Did the Apostles Die?" *NeverThirsty.org*. Accessed, 19 December 2021.
https://www.neverthirsty.org/bible-qa/qa-archives/question/how-did-the-apostles-die/.
Note: Given the antiquity of the subject, the accounts of the Apostle's deaths vary, not whether they were martyred for their friend Jesus, but the means by which they met death. My summary here reflects what seems to be the majority view.

Clearly, Jesus surrounded Himself with more than golfing buddies, bunko babes, or Sunday stalwarts.

Father God, may you please surround each of us with such a band of soul friends as our Older Brother enjoyed. Amen

Fishing together, playing cards, eating, drinking, traveling, reading, studying the Bible, and sitting by the fire are integral to friendship. However, they aren't the stuff of soul friendship as much as they are the settings in which soul friendship takes root and forms.

Friendships of the soul form during quality time. But you don't realize quality time unless you invest in quantities of time.

By all appearances, Jesus was thoughtful and strategic in selecting His immediate friends and His close friends like Mary, Martha, and Lazarus. You will recall that His friend Mary is the woman who anointed His feet with oil and His friend Lazarus is the man He raised from the dead. Scripture simply says, "Now Jesus loved Martha, and her sister, and Lazarus."[247]

Jesus' friends were a diverse, thoughtful, rowdy, unruly, and disparate collection of men and women. About the only thing His immediate friends had in common was that several of them knew how to fish. Group theorists would call them a heterogeneous group: a complex collection of unlikely compatriots.

Jesus chose this diverse assemblage to be His friends because He recognized that He was not a simple person.

---

[247] Cf.: John 11:5.

Given His complex soul, Jesus invited a diverse group to compliment His complexity.

As a human being, Jesus required friends for His soul. But not just any friends. Everyone wasn't capable of being a soul friend to Jesus. By choosing these twelve, He wasn't being exclusive; He was being realistic, about Himself, and His soul's needs. Lewis writes, "By myself I am not large enough to call the whole man into activity; I want other lights than my own to show all his facets."[248] MacDonald puts it this way: "I cannot grow into what God wants me to be (and do) unless I am in tight formation with some others."[249]

Jesus knew He needed friends to showcase and magnify Him fully. He surrounded Himself with likely candidates.

Jesus' friends helped Him demonstrate His complete self, the individual affirmed in our creed: "...existing fully as God, and fully as man, with a relational soul and human body."[250]

Jesus and His friends spent time—quantity time—together. There must have been copious campfires, long miles, and far more conversations than the Bible contains. Over time, interspersed midst the mundane, the magic of souls bonded together in soul friendship transpired. Jesus and the twelve

---

[248] Lewis, C.S. *The Four Loves*. Harcourt, Brace, and Company. New York, NY. 1960.

[249] MacDonald, Gordon. *A Resilient Life*. Thomas Nelson Publishers. Nashville, TN. 2004. Note: With his use of the phrase, "grow into what God wants me to be," the author is not referring to a progressively developing identity, rather the growth of character that exemplifies true identity within a resilient lifestyle. As he says later, "Living resiliently cannot be done alone." Being conveys the idea of essence: This is who I am. This is how I conduct myself, present myself, and comport myself as a child of God filled with the Spirit. This sense of being is progressive in that you increasingly understand and exemplify who you are, who God is, and what your relationship looks like throughout all aspects of life. As this reality is apprehended with greater clarity, which will occur most reliably through practice of the disciplines, your resiliency as a person increases.

[250] Editors. "The Athanasian Creed." *RCA.org*. Accessed, 19 December 2021. https://www.rca.org/about/theology/creeds-and-confessions/the-athanasian-creed/

became true friends—a soul-level network made strong in their diversity, shared experience, candid confession, and soul-searching reliance upon each other.

Now, let me be blunt: It is *not possible* to build soul friendship via social media, fleeting moments, and large-group events. These are either too limited, too shallow, too brief, too competitive, or too lacking in substance to give soul friendship even a fractional chance of forming.[251]

Long before the advent of social media, and even prior to mass urbanization, Henry David Thoreau observed that, "The mass of men lead lives of quiet desperation. What is called resignation is confirmed desperation. Unconscious despair is concealed even under what are called the games and amusements of mankind."[252]

In ancient and medieval times, it was believed that soul friendship was the purest and truest means to deeper and more joyful, genuine living. Apart from friendship, our predecessors observed that all of life required striving for survival and status. But in soul friendship, it was possible to get away from the stressors of life and rise to the heights of soul-fulfillment where gods and angels dwell.

The busy, demanding pace of today's lifestyle, including the *addictive*[253] demand of our devices, is an enemy to developing and practicing soul friendship. In fact, busyness

---

[251] If you have not watched and digested the Netflix documentary, "The Social Dilemma," you simply must devote 90-minutes to consider the subject. If you have not researched the effect of devices on human development and interaction, even a rudimentary search reveals that our devices are wrecking our humanity, creating schisms between us, while advancing false narratives about the world, culture, community, and individual self-awareness.

[252] Thoreau, Henry David. *Civil Disobedience and Other Essays*. Cricket House Books, LLC. Madison, WI. 2019.

[253] Editors. "Is Device Addiction a Thing?" *ReachOutRecovery*.com. July 2021. https://reachoutrecovery.com/what-is-digital-device-addiction/

is a deadly poison to soul-level friendship. And don't succumb to the rationalization that a telephone call to catch up or a reunion with old friends will provide the forums necessary to secure the bond of your soul to another's.

You can neither schedule nor shortchange the quality time in which soul friendship takes root. Quality time occurs serendipitously within copious quantities of time together.

As you can see, the spiritual practices of rest and soul friendship are complimentary. But not only these. In his explorations of how the Body of Christ functions together, Bonhoeffer writes in *Life Together* about how daily pace, shared meals, singing together, reading Scripture and other literature together, confession, and worship all formulate the cohesion of life together as a group and soul friendship among a smaller group.[254]

While Jesus was soul friends with the twelve and others, there was a tighter group of three—Peter, James, and John—with whom Jesus identified and connected even more deeply within His soul. Having three intimate soul friends doesn't make Jesus restrictive or selective, it demonstrates His humanity. The majority of people are mentally and emotionally incapable of having more than 3-5 intimate friends.[255]

Jesus' practice of the spiritual disciplines was not merely a demonstration of principles, it was a portrait of cohesive, thoughtful, integrated living. He understood that in order to realize and satisfy the desire of His heart, He needed to live

---

[254] Bonhoeffer, Dietrich. Ibid.

[255] Cf.: Editors. "How Many Friends Does the Average Person Have?" *GoodTherapy.org*. February 8, 2019. https://www.goodtherapy.org/blog/psychology-facts/how-many-friends-does-average-person-have-0208197

a disciplined life that advanced His freedom to communicate with God.

Specifically, by surrounding Himself with soul friends, Jesus was able to realize and convey with shining luster who He was, His priorities in life, and His purpose in living as the Light in a dark world. Jesus' friends facilitated for Him, themselves, and others the clarion message that He [Jesus] was indeed the way, the truth, and the life of God and to God.[256]

There is challenge in each of the disciplines. I suppose that's why they are called disciplines, and because they are challenging, they require practice. But for the record, I labor more with the basis of soul friendship than any of the other disciplines.

What is that basis? Time.

Soul friendship takes time.

Of course, the time required to form soul friendship is not onerous—or, it doesn't have to be. It just forces a decision that is both blessing and curse: Will I maintain my pace and fulfill the current demands I feel, or will I curtail other things and prioritize time to care for my soul with friends?

Not to beat a dead horse, but there is no substitute for quantity time. Without your generous investment of time, there is no chance for the quality time necessary to your soul's required friendships.

There are numerous enemies of your soul, and time management is a tricky business, especially if you work for

---

[256] Cf.: John 14:6.

others, or thinking specifically about parents, have dependent others who require your time. Not to sound indifferent, but you are not the first person to have these demands upon you that you endure. You are simply the latest. The spiritual practice of soul friendship remains a fundamental discipline of the faith.

The wisdom of Scripture, the counsel of those who preceded you, and the life of your Older Brother all bear testimony: It is to the benefit of your heart's desire to prioritize practicing the spiritual disciplines, including the time necessary to acquire, practice, and benefit from soul friendship.

Now, I would be remiss if I didn't return to an earlier point to look the tiger square in the eye: The greatest impediment to practicing this discipline is the device in your pocket or purse.

On average, people tap, swipe, or click their smartphone 2600 times per day. Over 70% of us sleep with our device. Depending on age, we send/receive between 70 and 110 texts per day and respond to each within 1-2 minutes.[257]

Each time your device displays an image or notification, your brain is rewarded with dopamine, the same chemical that converts cocaine users into addicts. Around 50% of

[257] Drah, Hermina. "30 Surprising Cell Phone Addiction Statistics for 2021." *DisturbMeNot.co*. January 15, 2021. https://disturbmenot.co/cell-phone-addiction-statistics/

smartphone users[258] believe they are addicted to their device—and the studies do not disagree.[259]

Nomophobia[260] is now a recognized mental illness: fear of being without a connected device. Since the advent of the smartphone in 2007, our attention span has degraded to *eight seconds.*

This means that every eight seconds, you are distracted while attempting to read your Bible, reflect, rest, be silent, or practice solitude. Every eight seconds, your worship is interrupted and your prayer derailed. Time with your friend is marginalized by your inability to pay attention, your compulsion to reach for your device, or your preference for the screen versus the person across from you.[261]

Unmanaged pace and unfiltered demand are enemies of your soul and your relationships. Barring your aggressive action to manage the busyness, noise, and interruptions, even "at rest" your life will be driven by distraction. Chief among the sources of this soul-withering concern is your ever-connected device.

Consider the ambitious aspiration of knowing God and understanding His mind. Contrast this against the allure of

---

[258] Editors. "44 Smartphone Addiction Statistics for 2021." *SlickText.com.* January 4, 2020. https://www.slicktext.com/blog/2019/10/smartphone-addiction-statistics/

[259] Pensworth, Luke. "Guide to Smartphone Addiction: Statistics, Symptoms, and Solutions." *DailyWireless.org.* May 11, 2020.
https://dailywireless.org/mobile/smartphone-addiction/

[260] Editors. "Smartphone Addiction." *HelpGuide.org.* Accessed, 19 December 2021. https://www.helpguide.org/articles/addictions/smartphone-addiction.htm

[261] Cf.: McKay, Brett and Kate. "Sunday Firesides: What's Happening Is...." *ArtofManliness.com.* December 18, 2021.
https://www.artofmanliness.com/character/behavior/sunday-firesides-whats-happening-is/

your device and other lifestyle demands. Ask yourself: Which of these fulfills the desire of my heart?

Note: I'm not asking you which of these you *want*. I'm asking you which you *desire*.

The practice of the spiritual disciplines puts you in position to realize your heart's desire, and the practice of soul friendship leverages your ability to realize your heart's desire sooner, and in more grandeur, than if you approach life alone.

Any impediment to your heart's desire, your devotion, or your ability to dedicate yourself to practice your spiritual disciplines is a distraction.

The practice of soul friendship is perhaps the most variable of the disciplines in that it is the only practice of the twelve that depends upon another person. Therefore, it is the most difficult discipline to manage and develop.

This said, there is profound consolation: Scripture states that God spoke with Moses as a friend and reminds us that Abraham was the friend of God. Like His first-born Son, our heavenly Father values friendship—your friendship.[262]

For all the fickleness of building soul-degree friends during this life, there is readiness in God to make you the friend of His soul in exchange for you making Him your soul friend.

How does soul friendship work?

"You will not find the warrior, the poet, the philosopher or the Christian by staring in his eyes as if he were your

---

[262] Cf.: Exodus 33:11; 2 Chronicles 20:7.

mistress: better fight beside him, read with him, argue with him, pray with him," wrote Lewis.[263]

The disciples learned, grasped, and loved Jesus and the way He lived. They each, and each in his eccentricities, became a unique friend, a true compadre, a soul friend. By being Jesus' friend, each became aware of character qualities otherwise unknown to them. And being possessed of such grit as to offer up his life as a reasonable respect for the friendship between their souls, they each did so.

But the disciples were not the only beneficiaries of soul friendship.

Jesus surrounded Himself with friends because He knew that as a man, He needed the benefit of trusted-others.

In a profound and remarkable turn, Jesus lived more fully, demonstrated grace more compellingly, walked with God more meaningfully, grew as an individual more robustly, progressed in His humanity more passionately, and flourished as a human being because of the contribution His soul-level friends made in His life.

Soul friends: Bonded. Sharing. Eating and drinking. Singing, struggling, celebrating, arguing, laboring, meditating, grieving, fighting together if they must, confessing, serving, loving, and *doing so together.*

This is the design and desire of God. He planted the same desire within you and designed practices to help you realize your desire. The practice of soul friendship accelerates your advancement. Distraction retards the realization of your heart's desire.

---

[263] Lewis. Ibid.

Questions and Considerations

1. This chapter presents Jesus' friends as a diverse group reflective of the diversity that characterized Jesus. Each of His friends brought something different to Jesus that brought to light a different aspect of Jesus' character. Given that you are Jesus' friend, what do you bring into your friendship with Him that demonstrates aspects of His character that would otherwise remain obscure? What aspects of your character does Jesus' friendship with you bring to light that would otherwise be obscure?

2. Who constitutes your cadre of soul friends? If you have a difficult time answering this question, which most in the West will, how will you go about building soul friendships? Whatever your answer, this is the most fundamental practice of the discipline of soul friendship. Similarly, with whom are you a soul-level friend? How do you nurture and protect and sustain this friendship? Finally, thinking about your answer to question 1, how do you go about fostering and developing your friendship with Jesus and how do you see Him making that same overture with you?

3. Toward the conclusion of this chapter, C.S. Lewis is quoted as saying, "You will not find the warrior, the poet, the philosopher or the Christian by staring in his eyes as if he were your mistress: better fight beside him, read with him, argue with him, pray with him." Who in your

THE SPIRITUAL PRACTICE OF SOUL FRIENDSHIP

life do you fight beside, read with, argue with, and pray with? If names come to mind, then these are most likely the people who qualify as your soul friends. If you don't have names, then you understand, a) that you need to find and develop these folks, and b) it tells you what sort of people you are looking for in your quest to establish soul friendship. Finally, do you and Jesus fight together, read together, argue, and discuss matters both large and small? He deeply desires your soul friendship, and truth be known, you deeply desire soul friendship with Him as well. You all are a match made in heaven. Your thoughts about this viewpoint?

SIXTEEN

The Spiritual Practice
of Service

> "
>
> *"Humility is nothing but truth, and pride is nothing but*
>
> *lying."*
>
> St. Vincent de Paul

Practicing service is not hard to define or illustrate.

Foster writes that you serve when you listen to someone, defend another's reputation, or hold the hand of a grieving soul. You serve when you prepare meals for the homeless during the holidays, when you work in the nursery at church, make a financial contribution, or sacrificially clean out your closets and deliver the goods for resale by the women's shelter.[264]

At its most basic, service is thinking of another's wellbeing first, ahead of looking out for yourself. Parenthood is therefore an act of service. So is holding the door for

---

[264] Cf.: Foster, Richard. "Understanding Service." *Renovare.org.* October 2014. https://renovare.org/articles/understanding-service

another. Teaching, advocating, recognizing, affirming: these are acts of service.

Service is noble, honorable, and thoughtful.

In its extreme, placing another ahead of yourself is what a hero does in laying down their life so another can live. We recognize heroism as an act of selfless courage and are offended when the heroes among us are disrespected.

Society increases in civility when greater and greater percentages of its citizens practice the Golden Rule: Do unto others as you would have them do unto you.[265]

This is desirable and good. While we might be amused by instances of incivility, no one who is healthy in their soul aspires to be uncivil, live in the toxic atmosphere of unkindness, or keep the company of a narcissist. Even a conversation infused primarily with first-person pronouns—I, me, my, mine—becomes tedious quickly.

If even an unbeliever aspires to a more civil society, then why does service to another, deference, and thinking of others before you think of yourself rise to the level of a spiritual discipline?

Technically, it is a correct answer to say, "I want to serve others because that's what Jesus did." True enough. In fact, Jesus said of Himself, "...the Son of Man did not come to be served, but to serve, and to give His life a ransom for many."[266]

---

[265] Cf.: Matthew 7:12.
[266] Matthew 20:28.

But why?

Why did Jesus demonstrate acts of service—and why does service rise to the level of a spiritual discipline for us?

Whether you are analyzing the seven deadly sins,[267] or the three, categorical sins listed in Scripture,[268] you can make an argument that the sin of pride is the most fundamental, and therefore, the most egregious, devious, deceptive, and most alluring. Scripture portrays pride as the first sin, both in heaven by Lucifer[269] and in the Garden by our predecessors.[270]

Thus, in your dedication to resist sin, the initial point of contact with the enemy of your soul is pride. Master pride, or prevent pride from penetrating your life, and you control the battlefields of your life.

It is not good enough to identify an individual who is consumed with pride and then dedicate yourself to not be like that person. The reason is that resisting a big pitfall leaves too much room for negotiation, rationalization, and tolerance of a lesser form of pride. You may as well vow not to get wet while walking on a rainy day and judge your success against the man walking without an umbrella. You both get wet.

The man who declares he's 99% humble reveals that he is 100% proud because he continues to believe that his worth, value, and standing as a person are based to some extent—

---

[267] Cf.: Editors. "Seven Deadly Sins." *Wikipedia.org*. Accessed, 19 December 2021. https://en.wikipedia.org/wiki/Seven_deadly_sins re.: lust, gluttony, greed, sloth, wrath, envy, pride.

[268] Cf.: 1 John 2:16 re. lust of the flesh, lust of the eye, and boastful pride of life.

[269] Cf.: Isaiah 14:13-14.

[270] Cf.: Genesis 3:1-24.

even to an nth degree—within himself and his sense of self-justification. Lewis writes in *The Four Loves*, "…this pretense that we have anything of our own or could for one hour retain by our own strength any goodness that God may pour into us, has kept us from being happy." He goes on to write, "The consequences of parting with our last claim to intrinsic freedom, power, or worth, are real freedom, power, and worth, really ours just because God gives them and because we know them to be (in another sense) not 'ours'."[271]

Any aspiration or effort to establish yourself, recognize yourself, or set yourself apart is a delusion of self-grandeur and self-entitlement—the conviction that you are owed, deserving, or intrinsically due recognition and identification by God and others.

Dedication to self-establishment plants the seed of pride, first within you, then with God, and then with others. Once rooted, an established sense of pride makes you vulnerable to the lusts that define all sins—all of which are germinated from the seed of pride.

Whether sin rewards you or embitters you, all sin is independence from God—and therein is the definition of pride.

Augustine said, "It was pride that changed angels into demons; it is humility that makes men as angels."

In the spiritual discipline of service, you practice, learn, and demonstrate humility. This is the rationale underlying this spiritual fundamental.

---

[271] Lewis. Ibid.

Both James and Peter state the same imperative: "Humble yourselves."[272] Paul offers a practical clue as to how humility happens: "Do nothing from selfishness or empty conceit, but with humility of mind regard one another as more important than yourselves; do not *merely* look out for your own personal interests, but also for the interests of others."[273]

Note that humility occurs in the mind. Thus, humility is an attitude, a decision, an outlook, a conviction, a manner of thinking indicative of your new self.

Paul tells the Believers located in Rome that they will be transformed by the renewing of their mind. He tells the Colossian Christians to set their mind on things above, not on earthly matters.[274]

Summing up, Paul writes: "Have this attitude in yourselves which was also in Christ Jesus, who, although He existed in the form of God, did not regard equality with God a thing to be grasped, but emptied Himself, taking the form of a bond-servant, *and* being made in the likeness of men. Being found in appearance as a man, He humbled Himself by becoming obedient to the point of death, even death on a cross."[275]

Paul instructs you to adopt the same attitude you observe in Jesus Christ. To this end, note that Jesus "humbled Himself," just as James and Peter exhort you to do.

Self-elevation, self-primacy, self-sufficiency, self-determination, self-worth, self-importance; me, myself, I.

---

[272] Cf.: James 4:10; 1 Peter 5:6.

[273] Philippians 2:3-4.

[274] Cf.: Romans 12:2; Colossians 3:1-4.

[275] Philippians 2:5-8.

Self-regard. Each of these terms and pronouns are indicative of pride and the pride of [my] life. Even a light embrace, or passive adoption, of self-entitlement makes you vulnerable to temptation.

How did Christ manage temptation?

He adopted an attitude of service, a humility of mind. Each day, in every way, Jesus knew that He came to serve, not be served. Thus, you not only have a window into your Older Brother's soul, but you see how He managed being tempted in all ways like you are... yet without succumbing to sin.[276]

The practice of the spiritual discipline of service protects you from temptation rooted in pride, reminds you that you bring nothing to God that is worth keeping—"for me, to live, is Christ"[277]—and reestablishes with every act of service that it is in losing your life that you find your life. While pride afflicts your ability to see clearly, humility raises your awareness of reality, especially what is true of you in your relationship with God.

Erwin McManus writes, "Humility is not about having a low self-esteem. Humility is about self-awareness."

The more a person understands the magnitude of God's grace, the more they realize what Lewis conveyed earlier: In candid self-awareness, you understand that you bring nothing to God. There is NO basis for your life, your esteem, or your standing apart from Jesus Christ. All that you are must be attributed to the mercy of God.

---

[276] Cf.: Hebrews 4:15.
[277] Philippians 1:21.

Understanding, adopting, and demonstrating this attitude, disposition, and conviction is pure, direct, unadulterated power. But this is the power of Christ in and through you. This is clear-headed self-awareness. That God would condescend to include you in the life of Christ is remarkable. Grasping even a whiff of this grace causes gratitude to overflow your soul and permeate your life.

It is a heady thing to be loved by God, to access His Scripture, grasp what is true, and enjoy eternal destiny. It is remarkable to be blessed by God. To be forgiven of your sin and sinfulness is empowering.

Practicing service protects you from any belief that you merit God's mercy, deserve heaven, or that you occupy an exalted position in life because of anything you've done. As Merton observed, "Pride makes us artificial; humility makes us real."

When you practice the discipline of service, your faith is made real—real as in relevant, compelling, loving. Indeed, faith-in-action. The world is not impressed by spiritual talk. The days of inviting people to church, and this having perceived value to outsiders, are past.

A drowning society is not interested in what you say while inside the brick and mortar of the church or your private cloister. A drowning society is desperate for a courageous soul who will come to where they are and rescue them. This is what God did in Jesus' incarnation—and as His ambassador, this is your calling and your representation of His life in you.

Jesus' final instruction was, "Go."[278] In the upper room, He endowed His followers with power to be His witnesses.[279]

While the spiritual practice of service guards your soul against pride and instills you with the safeguard of humility, your practice expresses love to those whom you serve. It's like Jesus said, "Greater love has no one than this, that one lay down his life for his friends."[280]

Herein is the benefit and bounty of practicing the spiritual discipline of service.

[278] Cf.: Matthew 28:19-20.
[279] Cf.: Acts 1:7-8.
[280] John 15:13.

Questions and Considerations

1. Once again, we encounter a discipline designed to guard us against the horrid sin of pride. With the practice of service, we are confronted with how secure we believe we are in Christ and the degree to which we are willing to lay our life down so another can flourish. Two questions then: First, are you practicing the discipline of service to others, and second, is your practice of service actively confronting the rudimentary temptation of pride? These are both yes-no questions, but the labor of analyzing them will serve you well while guarding you against self-delusion.

2. What is your understanding of where humility comes from and how it is developed?

3. The most rudimentary, yet most profound, act of service was captured by Jesus in one word: "Go!" Being loving and good, He would not tell you to go if you were not equipped to do so. Thus, what is your equipping? What does going look like for you? To be clear, I'm not asking what others expect you to do or what your church tells you "going" or serving look like. I'm asking you to consider how your heavenly Father has equipped you and how He is asking you to, "Go!" in your spiritual practice of service. Now, your thoughts?

Epilogue

Life is a bumping, herky-jerky, grinding journey along an irregular path. Any venue featuring more than a few folks is a messy and inefficient business. For this, there are leadership books, business books, and religious books.

But these irregularities are not the issues I'm addressing in this book.

While the church spins into irrelevancy and civil society veers toward chaos and societal breakdown, there are only two options large enough, knowing enough, and powerful enough to quell our concerns and fulfill our needs: institutionalized government or relationship with God.[281]

It is imminently clear that human institutions and governmental initiatives are insufficient to calm the storm and restore the peace and tranquility we desire. A November 2021 Pew Research Center study[282] is alarming. America is not divided between two groups: Red and Blue,

---

[281] Cf.: Gillham, Preston. "What Are We Thinking and What Must We Do?" *PrestonGillham.com*. July 16, 2021. https://www.prestongillham.com/blog/what-are-we-thinking-and-what-must-we-do

[282] Editors. "Beyond Red vs. Blue: The Political Typology." *PewResearch.org*. November 9, 2021. https://www.pewresearch.org/politics/2021/11/09/beyond-red-vs-blue-the-political-typology-2/

Conservative or Progressive. America is divided into nine, distinct groups the study reports.

Thus, we are not divided. We are fractured.

In his January 2021 inaugural address, President Biden pledged to bring unity to the country. Thirteen months into his term, our schisms are metastasizing and his polling numbers are plummeting. And while there is talk of change motivated by the mid-term elections, a realist realizes that a change in government does not ensure unity.

If your hope and future are tied to government, your hope and future are tenuous.

The alternative option belongs to God.

Of course, the Kingdom of God is unfazed by humanity's heaving and sighing, writhing and wriggling. The Christian comfort is that you are God's ambassador—His representative living in a foreign land, representing your true home. As the poet wrote, "This world is not my home, I'm just a-passing through, / My treasures are laid up somewhere beyond the blue; / The angels beckon me from heaven's open door, / And I can't feel at home in this world anymore."[283]

On the one hand, this assurance—this reassurance in spite of life's lunacy—gives you confidence, security, and eternal hope. On the other hand, this assurance equips you to engage this life. As you've read time-and-again in these chapters, Jesus told you that you are to be salt and light in a dark, collapsing, and increasingly petty society.

---

[283] Anonymous. "This World is Not My Home." *Library.TimelessTruths.org.* 1919. https://library.timelesstruths.org/music/This_World_Is_Not_My_Home/

As society unravels, stress escalates. As life grows uncertain, people become more desperate. Desperate people do desperate things—and desperation is not rational, reasonable, judicious, calculating, logical, or efficient.

Pew's political typology is telling: American society is no longer as stable as it once was. We are degenerating as a society and culture.

This should be—must be—our finest hour as a church. If only we can once again find our footing, summon our courage, and step into the dark waters of life and culture with the light of Christ.

I'm reminded of the story of Queen Esther, a Jewess living in Persia and married to the king, Ahasuerus (aka, Xerxes I). Unwittingly, Ahasuerus endorsed genocide of the Jews in Persia. As the evil plan proceeded, Esther's cousin and guardian, Mordecai, offered her counsel regarding a courageous appeal to her husband, Ahasuerus: Mordecai said to Esther, "For if you remain silent at this time, relief and deliverance will arise for the Jews from another place and you and your father's house will perish. And who knows whether you have not attained royalty for such a time as this?"[284]

No doubt, this must be the church's finest hour. Who knows but that for such a time as this, the church has been raised up?

Except that the church—generally speaking—has shot itself in the foot and is no longer in the fight for those lost in sin

---

[284] Esther 4:14.

and darkness. As I've written earlier, there are no good numbers associated with the church.

The broad view of why this has transpired is so complex as to be overwhelming—and overwhelmed people are resistant to change, even if their status quo is unproductive. While this is normal, Einstein (it's thought) was correct when he said, "The definition of insanity is doing the same thing over and over again and expecting a different result."

I was visiting with a close observer of the organized church. As we talked, his thoughts grew sober, his voice dropped, and he said, "When it comes to the future role of the church, I fear we are straightening deck chairs on the Titanic."

Remediating the church, breathing life back into her, feels overwhelming. Complex problems require complex solutions.

Unless....

Unless the problem only seems complex and is in reality a fundamental problem.

Fundamental problems require fundamental solutions. Said another way, a fundamental problem cannot be resolved programmatically and cannot be remedied stylistically. You fix a fundamental problem by returning to the practice of your fundamentals.

Thus, the rationale for this collection of chapters exploring the fundamentals of faith: the spiritual disciplines.

Now, our exploration, evaluation, and examination of *Rigorous Grace* is concluded.

Contemplating his incarceration into the Nazi concentration camps that imprisoned him at Theresienstadt, Auschwitz, and others, his family murdered and his life's work destroyed, Viktor Frankl isolated what he identified as the last freedom: his free will.

In between the various stimuli that come haphazard and uninvited into your life, and your response to these stimuli, there is a space occupied by the freedom to choose how you will respond. Frankl's revelation was that not even the Nazi's and their horrid holocaust could steal this last freedom unless he voluntarily relinquished it to them.

Thus, in between stimulus and response there is ability—the ability to choose your response. Literally, Frankl identified and embraced the last freedom of response-ability: responsibility.

In these pages, I've attempted to stir you, inspire you, stimulate your soul, and compel you by making you aware. I've advocated for a particular response: a diligent return to practicing the spiritual disciplines of the Christian life.

The advantage now rests with you. What will your response to these pages be? What will you determine your response-ability—your responsibility—to be given these chapters?

To paraphrase Mordecai, "Who knows whether you have not attained royalty as a child of God for such a time as this?

How to Become a Christian

The key to any relationship, even a relationship with God, is mutual respect. While I could write pages and pages on mutual respect and relationships, the point of this appendix is to consider relationship with God, i.e. becoming a Christian, a follower of Jesus Christ, a disciple of His, or simply, a Believer.

When God made you, He endowed you with an independent, free will. Certainly, God will be persuasive, as any strong individual will be with their perspective, but out of respect for your self-determination, He will not force Himself upon you. If you and He are going to have a relationship, it will only be because you both agree of your own volition to enter into relationship.

In this book, I've likened this to marriage. It's an apt parallel. Both must agree and say "I do" to have a marriage.

God went to great lengths to make relationship possible. He did this by taking on humanity and coming to live among humankind. We know this event as Christmas, or the Incarnation, and recognize the person as Jesus Christ.

God took it upon Himself—as and through Jesus Christ—to remove all impediments that would preclude you and Him from enjoying a viable, vibrant, and vital relationship. All that was wrong, He made right. All that could go wrong, He made provision for. All of this, He accomplished in and through Jesus Christ.

The Bible verbalizes it like this: In your independence, you fall short of God's standard, i.e. you sin. In your humanity, you are flawed as the descendant of a flawed progenitor and race.[285] Said another way, you fall short and sin, and by nature, you are a sinner.

Two problems stand between you and God, and a relationship: a) your sinful performance and b) your identity as a sinner.

So, becoming a Christian and being accepted by God is not simply being forgiven for the things you do wrong. You also need to be remade. Jesus said it like this: You need a new Father, a new life. You have to be born again in order to be part of a new family.[286]

Through Jesus Christ, God made provision for your poor performance (sins, in biblical parlance). Through Jesus Christ, God does away with your old identity (sin, the Bible calls it) and promises you a new identity as His child, i.e. forgiveness for what you've done and who you are.

There is only one thing standing between you and God. The one thing is you, or more specifically, your independent choice to accept His offer or remain a free agent. Recall my conversations with my atheist neighbor: He chose unfaith. I chose faith. Both of us made choices regarding how we would approach life and eternity.

The mutual respect aspect of this relationship looks like this: God will not violate your freedom of choice, but He will make a provision to remove everything standing between you and Him. Your part is: a) agreeing with Him about needing Him, and

---

[285] Romans 3:23; 5:12-21.
[286] John 3:1-8.

b) asking that He enter your life, forgive you of your sins and sinfulness, and give you new life.[287]

It's that simple.

To be clear though: Before becoming a Christian, you should make certain you understand that you are not simply buying a life insurance policy that ensures you go to heaven when you die and have your sins forgiven in this life. That's shortsighted. More than that, it's disrespectful, thereby calling into question your motive in the first place.

A relationship that is mutually respectful is a relationship committed to daily life together (more about this in a moment). If God simply wanted you in heaven, He would make it so. But He desires more than to populate heaven. He desires a relationship.

The question is, do you as well?

If so, here's your next step: Discussing things with God is called prayer. Here's a simple statement you can make to God (in prayer). I promise you that He will hear your prayer, take you at your word, set things right between the two of you, and make you part of His family:

> Lord God, thank you for hearing me as I pray. I'm coming to begin a relationship with you—the relationship you so generously offer. I've lived independently of you until now. But now, I relinquish being in charge of my own life and humbly ask you to forgive me where I've failed you and others. Would you make me your child, part of your eternal family? Would you make me a new person and begin your work in my life? I ask that you take charge

---

[287] Cf.: John 1:12; Romans 10:8-10; Acts 16:31 (esp. vss. 22-34).

and sit on the throne of my life. I recognize you as my Lord and God. I want you to live in me and I want to live in and through you. Thank you, Amen.

If you prayed this prayer, I encourage you to reference the following pages for resources to encourage, guide, and facilitate your heart's desire to know God and walk with Him.

What Now?

Here are some suggested next steps designed to help you mature in the relationship you've begun with God.

As I mentioned in the chapter, "The Spiritual Practice of Reading the Bible," I suggest you purchase one of the Bible versions referenced in the chapter and begin reading the Gospel of John. You can locate it in the Table of Contents in your Bible. It does a great job of introducing you to Jesus Christ. Once read, I recommend you read the Book of Ephesians next. It does a great job of introducing you to the new you.

I urge you to make reading a selection from the Bible a regular feature of each day. It would be best if you stayed in the New Testament until you get your spiritual feet underneath you. If you would like guidance on what to read each day, I refer you to YouVersion.com and their daily reading plan.

In addition to the Bible, I recommend you read *Lifetime Guarantee* by Bill Gillham. It will help you understand more about the spiritual transaction between you and God, what that means for your new identity, and offer practical applications that I believe will be advantageous to you.

To grasp more of God's perspective on His relationship with you, I suggest you read Malcolm Smith's book, *The Power of the Blood Covenant*. Your takeaway will be how serious God is about never releasing His grip on you.

Both Malcolm and Bill have audio resources that you can search and access.

If you've enjoyed this book and would like to subscribe, I write a blog. You can subscribe at PrestonGillham.com.

A place where you can meet other Believers is vital to your spiritual growth. Finding an appropriate church is important. I say "appropriate" because all churches are not equal. Locating a church is sort of like finding a new friend. Not all available are suitable, but many can be. Similarly, if you attend a prospective church and it just doesn't feel right, try another.

Churches come in a liberal variety and conservative variety. This is not liberal versus conservative like in politics, but liberal versus conservative in the way they view the Bible and Christianity.

Liberal churches and denominations have departed a conservative approach to Christianity and the Bible and adopted a socially liberal view instead. It will be difficult for you to grow in your Christian faith in one of these churches for the simple reason that they don't talk about the Bible, faith in Christ, and spiritual growth as much as they talk about social initiatives. While it's not possible to be categorical, Methodist, Disciples of Christ (also called Christian), Episcopal, and many Presbyterian churches are liberal leaning.

On the conservative side of things, churches called Bible churches, e.g. "XYZ" Bible Church, most Baptist, and some Presbyterian churches are conservative leaning. These are likely a good choice for you to look into because you will hear messages, and have access to programs, that will help you grow in your faith and be confident in your walk with Christ.

While this sounds overwhelming, the litmus test is simple and reliable: Does the church view the Bible—all of it—as the inspired, infallible Word of God? If so, you're good to go. If they flinch when you ask this question, keep looking.

If Bible Study Fellowship (BSF) or Community Bible Study (CBS) are near you, these are solid sources for you to access.

How do you know or find out what a church or Christian group believes?

Many have statements of their faith or beliefs on their websites. You can also call and ask about their view of the Bible. If they hedge, keep looking. The first step in the right direction will be the church that has a ready, clear, and concise statement of their belief about the Bible as the inspired Word of God, as opposed to a word of God, or containing the word of God, and so forth.

As of this writing, here are some current teachers you can listen to (and read) for teaching and guidance: Andy Stanley, Ralph Harris, Tim Chalas, Frank Friedmann, Malcolm Smith, Timothy Keller, Tony Evans, and Andrew Farley. If you prefer a female perspective, I suggest Beth Moore, Kay Arthur, Lysa TerKeurst, and Priscilla Shirer.

I also refer you to my writings and books. You can find both at: PrestonGillham.com.

In the "Suggested Resources" of this book, I suggest additional resources to help you ground your faith.

Suggested Resources

PrestonGillham.com
Each week I write a blog article regarding faith, culture, and the intersection of the two. You can subscribe for free and the article will automatically deliver to the email address of your choosing. In addition, everything regarding my work, some of my life, and a lot of history are at this site. Click the "Follow" button to subscribe.

Swagger—**Preston Gillham**
Swagger: Keeping Your Wits When Others are Not is a collection of essays on thought, life, and belief. The world is a tough, irregular place. Cultural chaos. Noise. Tumult. Confusion. It's disorienting. Lose your wits and you'll find your life, beliefs, and convictions unravel. *Swagger* is for the courageous. Each essay tackles a relevant topic. Each essay tackles today. Even if turbulence persists, those with swagger maintain their poise and composure.

No Mercy— **Preston Gillham**
No Mercy is a sweeping adventure of life, love, trust, and desire - a portrait of the spiritual battle between flesh and spirit, an odyssey asserting that real   life is more than meets the eye.

Hank Henderson thought he was going on vacation to Montana, but his brother had something else in mind. Hank's life soon dangles on the precipice of disaster.

Disoriented. Injured. His resources depleted, Hank is caught between powerful forces. One is dark, aggressive, and powerful. The other, of questionable integrity, appears Hank's only option for freedom.
From his placid fishing of Malden Creek into a dungeon of double-dealing. Hank crosses swollen rivers, scales blizzard strewn heights, and discovers more than he bargained for in an unlikely ally.

His hope dependent upon a hesitant trust, Hank gambles to emerge from *No Mercy* a transformed person.

Battle for the Round Tower— Preston Gillham
Preston Gillham takes us again into the true world of spiritual life via his novel, *Battle for the Round Tower*.

Returning to Gnarled Wood after two years away, Hank Henderson discovers that the risks have risen. He encounters a dark, spiritual world of subterfuge, black operations, and intrigue.

Powerful beyond what he realizes, Hank wrestles with distrust and doubt to become the man of his destiny.

Through the characters he creates, Preston shows us a powerful people called Believers and Christ-followers.

Confident Woman— Anabel Gillham
God does not call women to be perfect. He wants them to be confident—confident in His love and acceptance.

Lifetime Guarantee— Bill Gillham

A witty, humorous, and candid book about living as a Christian, what goes wrong, how to remedy your upsets, and your true identity in Christ.

The Reason for God— Timothy Keller
Addresses the frequent doubts that skeptics, and even ardent believers, have about religion. Using literature, philosophy, real-life conversations, and potent reasoning, Keller explains how the belief in a Christian God is, in fact, a sound and rational one.

Mere Christianity— C.S. Lewis
The most important writer of the 20th century explores the unequaled opportunity for Believers and nonbelievers alike to consider his powerful apologetic for the Christian faith.

A Resilient Life—Gordon MacDonald
It makes little difference how fast you can run the 100 meters when the race is 400 meters long. Life is not a sprint; it is a distance run, and it demands the kind of conditioning that enables people to go the distance.

More Than a Carpenter— Josh McDowell
A brief book of less than 100 pages exploring the Bible, the resurrection, and Christianity.

The Power of the Blood Covenant— Malcolm Smith
One message exists to transform the Body of Christ in the twenty-first century: Unraveling the mystery of God's eternal oath.

The Case for Christ— Lee Strobel
Strobel cross-examines a dozen experts from schools such as Cambridge, Princeton, and Brandeis, asking hard-hitting questions—and building a captivating case for Christ's divinity.

Is God Speaking to Me?—Lysa TerKeurst

Living with a deeper awareness of God's leading isn't just for a select few—it's for you too! Written especially for women, but plenty of principles for men as well.

The Jesus I Never Knew— Philip Yancey

Presents a complex character who generates questions as well as answers; a disturbing and exhilarating Jesus who wants to radically transform your life and stretch your faith. Uncovers a Jesus who is brilliant, creative, challenging, fearless, compassionate, unpredictable, and ultimately satisfying.

Suggested Websites

Biblegateway.com
Access and locate resources to study the Bible, search for Scriptures, and explore biblical subjects. Almost every translation of the Bible is readable and searchable.

Lifetime.org
Listen and read about your true identity in Christ and how to live an effective, dynamic life as a Christian.

Network220.org
Locate Christian organizations in your area who teach, train, and guide your walk with Christ and true identity in Him. A good resource for conferences, additional materials, and finding a local church. Organized by States in alphabetical order.

OurResoluteHope.com
This site is the teaching ministry of Pastor Frank Friedmann. Frank is an exegetical Bible teacher—meaning, he teaches the Scripture verse-by-verse, often word-by-word. He is a reliable theologian, intensely practical, honest, transparent, and imminently qualified to speak into your life.

PrestonGillham.com

Read more about Preston, his work, life, and thoughts on life and leadership. This site has an extensive archive of Preston's writing. Subscribe to his blog and stay close to what Preston offers for today's issues from his walk with God. Preston is a therapist and historian by training, a philosopher at heart, but mostly a fly fisherman with only occasional rivers to fish.

TimothyKeller.com

Tim Keller is a reliable biblical scholar who is a pastor at heart—meaning, he is easy to listen to, practical, and very relevant. He is a brilliant man who readily digests complex concepts and puts them forward for consumption in approachable language. His theology is reformed, which differs from other teachers in this suggested reading list, but that's okay. What Tim teaches is rock-solid reliable. He and his wife, Kathy, also have resources on marriage.

YouVersion.com

This site offers you daily reading plans to help you get started reading the Bible. They also offer discipleship materials, encouraging stories, and a robust app for your device.

The Battle for Your Soul

As you read while considering the place confession plays in your spiritual formation, it is important for your confession to be accurate and specific. By defining exactly what you are confessing, you are able to better assess and evaluate your successes, failures, and how God works specifically in meeting your needs, answering your prayers, and providing the power you need through His Spirit.

In this chapter, you will find two work sheets: 1) "The Flesh Inventory" and 2) "My True Identity in Christ." Each has instructions to guide you. The goal is to identify the unique ways in which Satan attempts to deceive you and the unique ways in which Father God provides truth to counter your temptation so that you live more consistent with your heart's desire.

Although you are a Christian and desire to please God, you experientially find that it is deceptively easy to live contrary to your heart's desire and your true self, i.e., you sin against God and live hypocritically to your true person. This is not uncommon. In fact, Paul wrote about his struggle with this in Romans 7:14-25.

This struggle you experience is the conflict between walking after the flesh versus in the power of the spirit (ref. Gal. 5:16-17). The reason temptation is so compelling is that your temptations correlate with your habitual patterns for living independent from God, i.e., what the Bible terms, your flesh: habitual patterns for thinking, feeling, choosing, and behaving contrary to God's truth.

For your faith and Scripture to be relevant, your challenge is to specifically identify your fleshly patterns, recognize when you are tempted to walk after the flesh, renounce that temptation, and set your mind on specific Scriptural truth that is the antidote to your specific temptation. Once you begin practicing what is true, a) you spend less time walking after what is not true, while b) creating new habit patterns for thinking, feeling, choosing, and behaving based upon what is true. In time, you will experience the habit patterns you hate weaken and the habit patterns for truth become more dominant and pervasive. In this way, you are transformed by the renewing of your mind (ref. Rom. 12:1-2).

Take your time with the two worksheets. Ask your heavenly Father to guide you. If you need additional input, I've provided resources for you to investigate.

The Flesh Inventory

These traits are patterns of your thought, emotion, and behavior and comprise your flesh, not your identity. Some of the traits are acceptable, some are not. These traits do not define you, nor do they determine who you are as a follower of Jesus Christ. Remember: We do not recognize ourselves by the flesh (ref.: 2 Cor 5:16).

Guide: Rate the traits with which you can identify on a scale from 1 – 10. Make 10 the highest/strongest rating. If you would prefer to download a separate worksheet as opposed to marking your book, you may do so at: Preston.Gillham.com/downloads.

Flesh Trait	Rate 1–10	Flesh Trait	Rate 1–10
Abused		Blame others	
Addiction		Boastful	
Achievement-based acceptance of yourself		Bossy	
Achievement-based acceptance of others		Bulimia	
Angry at God		Cannot apologize	
Angry at others		Cannot express gratitude	
Angry at yourself		Cannot keep a secret	
Anorexia		Capable	
Anxiety		Cause dissention	
Argumentative		Coldhearted/Lacking Compassion	
Astrology/Horoscopes/Occult		Competent	
Avoid intimacy		Complacent	
Arrogant		Compulsion to repay favors	
Bigotry (intolerant of others if different)		Compulsive behavior	
Bitterness		Compulsive thoughts	
Blame God		Conceit	

Flesh Trait	Rate 1–10	Flesh Trait	Rate 1–10
Control others		Fearful	
Controlled by emotions		Feel used	
Controlled by peers		Feel you don't matter	
Covetous		Gaslight others	
Deceitful/Sneaky		Gluttony	
Defensive		Gossip	
Demanding of others		Greed	
Demanding of your rights		Guarded/Not transparent	
Demanding of yourself		Guilt (legitimate)	
Demoralized		Guilt (unwarranted)	
Denial		Happiness is a major goal	
Depression		Harsh	
Despair		Hatred	
Despondent		Hostile toward yourself	
Devalued		Idolatry	
Difficult to receive help		Helpless	
Difficult to receive praise		Homosexual attraction	
Disappointment		Hostile toward God	
Discouragement		Hostile toward others	
Dismissed		Indulgence/If it feels good, do it	
Dismissive		Impatient	
Dissatisfied		Impulsive/Rash	
Distant or aloof		Impure thoughts	
Distrust		Inadequate	
Divisive		Incompetent	
Dominant		Independent	
Do not belong		Indifferent to other's pain	
Do not listen		Inferior	
Do not matter		Inhibited emotionally	
Do not trust God		Insecure	
Doubt		Insensitive	
Doubt Scripture		Insignificant	
Drink alcohol too much		Intelligent	
Drink to relax		Intemperance	
Driven		Internet/connectivity dependence	
Drug dependency		Intimidate others deliberately	
Entitled		Introspective	
Envy		Irrelevant	
Escapism		Jealousy	
Exceptional abilities		Lacking close friends	
False modesty		Lacking joy	
Fear of weakness		Lacking peace	

Flesh Trait	Rate 1–10	Flesh Trait	Rate 1–10
Lacking personal value		Pollyannaish	
Lacking personal viability		Pornography	
Lacking recognition		Possessive of others	
Laziness		Possessive of things	
Lonely		Prejudice	
Loner		Presumptuous	
Lots of friends		Pride	
Low self-discipline		Procrastination	
Lust for pleasure		Profane	
Lust for recognition		Project blame (aka, Gaslighting)	
Lust for sex		Prone to gossip	
Manipulate others		Racist	
Materialistic		Rebellious	
Misandry (hatred toward men)		Recognized or accomplished	
Misogyny (hatred toward women)		Rejected	
Must be in control		Religious	
Must be strong		Resentment	
Nagging		Restless	
Narcissism/It's all about me		Rigid or uncompromising	
Negativism		Right-ness, i.e., must be right	
Neglected		Sadness	
Nervousness		Screen or device dependence/addiction	
Niggling		Self-absorbed	
Not submissive to authority		Self-centered	
Obsessive-compulsive		Self-condemnation	
Over-committed/Too Busy		Self-confident	
Over-compensation		Self-deprecation/Self-depreciation	
Over-eating		Self-gratification	
Overly ambitious		Self-hatred	
Overly opinionated		Self-indulgence	
Overly sensitive to criticism		Self-justification	
Overly quiet		Self-pity	
Overly submissive		Self-reliant	
Passive		Self-righteous	
Passive aggressive		Self-serving	
People pleasing		Self-sufficient	
Perfectionism		Selfish ambition	
Performance-based acceptance of others		Selfish attitude	
Performance-based acceptance of yourself		Selfish with possessions	
Petty		Selfish with time	
Pity		Sensuality	
Pitiful		Sexual anger	

Flesh Trait	Rate 1-10	Flesh Trait	Rate 1-10
Sexual doubt		Undisciplined	
Sexual fantasizing		Unemotional	
Sexual fluidity		Unfeeling	
Sexual frustration		Ungrateful	
Sexual lust		Unimportant	
Sexual resentment		Unloved	
Shameful/shame/shamed		Unlovely	
Skilled		Unreasonable standards for others	
Slovenly		Unreasonable standards for yourself	
Sought after		Untrusting	
Stupid		Use of blackmail to control	
Subjective		Use of guilt to control	
Suicidal thinking		Use of manipulation to control	
Superior		Use of money to control	
Suppress emotions		Use of shame to control	
Suspicious of God		Use others	
Suspicious of others		Use of passivity to escape	
Talented		Use of threat to control	
Talk too much		Vanity	
Temper		Weak	
Too quick to speak		Withdrawal/withdrawn	
Transgender or LGBTQ+ Attraction		Workaholic	
Unaccepted		Worry	
Unbelief		Worthless	
Unemotional			

The fleshly characteristics with numerical ratings of 7-10 are your strongest, most problematic fleshly patterns; your besetting sins. Scripture calls these patterns "strongholds" or "fortresses" (ref.: 2 Cor. 10:3-6).

Now, reference the sheet "My True Identity" and look for Scriptures that address your besetting, fleshly patterns, i.e., the 7-10 habitual patterns. These verses are the spiritual antidote to your temptations. For example: If you put a 7-10 beside "self-condemnation," you will note that Romans 8:1 says that you are not condemned. If you put a 7-10 beside "worthless," you will note that 1 Corinthians 6:20 and 7:23 say that you are a person of tremendous worth because you have been bought with a price, i.e., Jesus Christ. As you consistently set your mind on the truth about your identity from Scripture, you will begin to see your struggles with sin and temptation diminish and come more under the control of the Holy Spirit. This process is what Romans 12:2 calls being transformed by the renewing of your mind. For more regarding the importance of setting your mind on what is true of you spiritually, ref.: Colossians 3:1-4 and Philippians 4:8-9.

For a more complete examination of the "Flesh Inventory," see *Lifetime Guarantee* by Bill Gillham. For an in-depth study of fleshly dynamics in a novel, see *No Mercy* by Preston Gillham. Both are available via Amazon.com. *Battle for the Round Tower* by Preston Gillham further examines overcoming the flesh. Preston's book, *Rigorous Grace: Practicing the Spiritual Disciplines*, guides how you develop spiritually.

To subscribe to Preston Gillham's blog and to explore his archives and books, visit: PrestonGillham.com.

For archives as well as written, audio, and video resources from Lifetime Ministries, visit: Lifetime.org.

My True Identity in Christ

Guide: Using the Scriptures below, and others you discover in the Bible, look for verses that are the antidote to the fleshly patterns you identified on *The Flesh Inventory* and rated from 7-10. By setting your mind on what is true of you spiritually (ref.: Phil. 4:8-9; Col. 3:2), you will spend less time walking after your fleshly patterns, more time with what is true of you, all while building new habits for how you think, feel, and behave that are based on truth, not deception.

John 1:12	I am a child of God (Rom. 8:16).
John 15:1,5	I am a branch, a channel of Christ's life to bear the fruit He produces.
John 15:15	I am Christ's friend.
John 15:16	I am chosen and appointed by Christ.
John 16:27	I am loved by my Father.
Acts 1:8	I am a personal witness of Christ for Christ.
Rom. 3:24	I am redeemed.
Rom. 5:1	I am justified and am at peace with God.
Rom. 6:1-6	I am free from the power of sin's rule over me.
Rom. 6:7	I have been freed from sin's power over me.
Rom. 6:18	I am a slave of righteousness—wholly dedicated to righteousness.
Rom. 6:22	I am enslaved to God—bound to Him with an inseparable bond.
Rom. 8:1	I am forever free from condemnation.
Rom. 8:14	I am a son of God. God is my "Papa" or "Dad" (Gal. 3:26, 4:6, Rom. 8:15).
Rom. 8:17	I am an heir of God and a fellow heir with Christ.
Rom. 11:16	I am holy.

Rom. 15:7	I am accepted. Christ accepts me.
I Cor. 1:2	I have been sanctified.
I Cor. 1:30	I am in Christ. He is my wisdom, righteousness, sanctification, and redemption.
I Cor. 2:12	I have received the Holy Spirit that I might know the things given to me by God.
I Cor. 2:16	I have the mind of Christ.
I Cor. 3:16	I am the temple (home) of God; His Spirit (His Life) dwells in me (I Cor. 6:19).
I Cor. 6:17	I am joined to the Lord and am one Spirit with Him.
I Cor. 6:19-20	I have been bought with a price; I am not my own; I belong to God.
I Cor. 12:27	I am a member of Christ's body (Eph. 5:30).
II Cor. 1:21	I am established in Christ and anointed by God.
II Cor. 2:14	I am victorious. God always leads me in His triumph in Christ.
II Cor. 3:17	I have liberty because of Christ.
II Cor. 5:14-15	I no longer live for myself, but for Christ.
II Cor. 5:17	I am a new creation.
II Cor. 5:18-19	I am reconciled to God and am a minister of reconciliation.
II Cor. 5:21	I am the righteousness of God in Christ.
Gal. 2:20	The old me was crucified. Christ lives in [the new] me; my life is Christ's life.
Gal. 4:6-7	I am a child of God and God's heir.
Eph. 1:1	I am a saint (I Cor. 1:2, Phil. 1:1, Col. 1:2).
Eph. 1:3	I am blessed with every spiritual blessing.
Eph. 1:4	I was chosen in Christ before the foundation of the world, holy and blameless.
Eph. 1:7-8	I have been redeemed, forgiven and am a recipient of His lavish grace.
Eph. 2:5	I have been made alive together with Christ.
Eph. 2:6	I have been raised up and seated with Christ in heaven.
Eph. 2:10	I am God's workmanship, created in Christ to do good work.
Eph. 2:13	I have been brought near to God.
Eph. 2:18	I have direct access to God through the Holy Spirit.
Eph. 2:19	I am a fellow citizen with the saints and a member of God's household.
Eph. 3:6	I am a fellow heir, a member of Christ, and a fellow partaker of God's promises.
Eph. 3:12	I may approach God with boldness and confidence.
Eph. 4:24	I am righteous and holy.
Phil. 3:20	I am a citizen of heaven.
Phi. 4:7	I have peace. God's peace guards my heart and my mind.
Phil. 4:19	I am cared for. God will supply all my needs-physical, psychological, & spiritual.
Col. 1:13	I am delivered from the domain of darkness and transferred to God's Kingdom.
Col. 1:14	I am redeemed and forgiven; the debt against me is cancelled (Col. 2:13-14).

MY TRUE IDENTITY IN CHRIST

Col. 1:27	I have the Spirit of Christ Himself in me.
Col. 2:7	I am firmly rooted in Christ and am now being built up and established in Him.
Col. 2:10	I have been made complete in Christ.
Col. 2:11	I am spiritually circumcised; my old, unregenerate nature has been removed.
Col. 2:12,13	I have been buried, raised, and made alive with Christ and am totally forgiven.
Col. 3:1	I have been raised up with Christ.
Col. 3:3	[The old] has died and my [present] life is now hidden with Christ in God.
Col. 3:4	I am alive and not alone. Christ is now my life.
Col. 3:12	I am chosen by God, holy and dearly loved (Acts 10:15).
I Thess. 5:5	I am a child of light, not of darkness.
II Tim. 1:7	I have been given a spirit of power, love, and discipline.
II Tim. 1:9	I am saved and set apart according to God's purpose and grace (Titus 3:5).
Heb. 2:11	I have honor. I am sanctified and one with Christ. God is not ashamed of me.
Heb. 3:1	I am a holy partaker of a heavenly calling.
Heb. 3:14	I am a partaker of Christ.
Heb. 4:16	I may come boldly before God to receive mercy and find grace to help me.
Heb. 10:10	I have been sanctified by His will (Acts 10:15).
I Pet. 2:5	I am a living stone, being built up (along with other saints) as a spiritual house.
I Pet. 2:9-10	I am chosen, part of a royal priesthood, a holy nation, God's own possession.
I Pet. 2:11	I am an alien and stranger to this world where I live temporarily.
II Pet. 1:4	I have been given Gods' promises. I am a partaker of God's divine nature.

To subscribe to Preston Gillham's blog and to explore his archives and books, visit: PrestonGillham.com.

For archives as well as written, audio, and video resources from Lifetime Ministries, visit: Lifetime.org.

If you would like to download a separate worksheet for easier reference, you may do so at: PrestonGillham.com/downloads.

Acknowledgements

Lindsay Inman: Thank you for your proofreading, design, layout, and diligent care in giving *Rigorous Grace* a compelling appearance.

Abe Martinez: Thank you for editing the audio version of *Swagger*. Because of your diligence and professionalism, the book sounds great.

Lazarus Media Productions: Thank you for your cover design and publication counsel. I appreciate and value your partnership.

Many thanks to my neighbor, Polly Hooper, for the back cover photo.

Contact Information and Bulk Pricing

Bonefish Publication

2020 Wilshire Blvd

Fort Worth, TX 76110

817-585-4185

Info@BonefishPublication.com

PUBLICATION ™